Search for the Authentic

Search for the Authentic

Navigating the Currents of Life
for Meaning and Purpose

DAVID SIKORRA

RESOURCE *Publications* • Eugene, Oregon

SEARCH FOR THE AUTHENTIC
Navigating the Currents of Life for Meaning and Purpose

Copyright © 2021 David Sikorra. All rights reserved. Except for brief quotations in critical publications or reviews, no part of this book may be reproduced in any manner without prior written permission from the publisher. Write: Permissions, Wipf and Stock Publishers, 199 W. 8th Ave., Suite 3, Eugene, OR 97401.

Resource Publications
An Imprint of Wipf and Stock Publishers
199 W. 8th Ave., Suite 3
Eugene, OR 97401

www.wipfandstock.com

PAPERBACK ISBN: 978-1-6667-1601-6
HARDCOVER ISBN: 978-1-6667-1602-3
EBOOK ISBN: 978-1-6667-1603-0

11/18/21

This work of love is dedicated to the one who helped it become so, my wife Sweet, who through her dedicated support through trials, tribulations, and triumphs was steadfastly at my side to support me in my quest and search for the *Authentic*.

Contents

Acknowledgments		ix
Introduction		xi

Part I | Exploring the Path of Life

1	On your Mark, Get Set, Go!	3
2	Becoming by Failing	8
3	Belonging with an Identify Built on Dust	14
4	Growing Pains and Growing Up	19
5	Prison and the Pursuit of a Dream	24
6	Running Again . . . To Escape	31
7	Moving Forward into Mission and Imagination	35
8	Charging Forward, to Make a Mark	39
9	Local Crooks Set the Course	43

Part II | The Enchanted Land

10	Making a Move	51
11	Return Trip Back Around the Planet	61
12	Recalling Beauty not Lost in Living	65
13	A Beauty to Rescue	71

Part III | Change, Challenge, and Conquest

14	Suffering Haiti, A History and Culture of Discord	79
15	The Early Modern Era	89
16	Expansion and Dysfunction	96
17	A Current of Sweet Grace and Relief from Grief	101
18	Could have Been Fiction . . . But it Wasn't	111
19	Open the Windows and Let the Fresh Air In	116

20	Earning the Title "Kingpin" Requires Being Best in the Trade	122
21	Misplaced Hope	130
22	The Capture and The Challenge	138
23	Fall Out from Folly	145
24	Eliobert, Kingpin Round Two	150
25	The Mountain, the Smoke and the Fire	156
26	A Dream Come True, a Country Changed	163

Part IV | *In Search of the Unseen; Locating that Pearl of Great Value*

| 27 | Life After Slaying the Dragon | 175 |
| 28 | The Challenge | 180 |

Bibliography   189

Acknowledgments

I wish to give special thanks to Wilkie Au, Professor Emeritus, Department of Theological Studies, Loyola Marymount University, for his immeasurable help and guidance in bringing me to the place which led me to take on this project; as well as his immense assistance in putting it in order. My gratitude runs through and over these pages.

Also, to my brother Joe, who's relentless and optimistic encouragement finally led me to sit down and attempt to take on the task of writing the memoire; beginning with random, disconnected memories, to a story that must be told. He made me believe.

Introduction

This is a story about a lifelong search for that which is the Authentic, the Truth, and the Reality behind the reason for which I was made. Not just me but every human being who searches for meaning in life, for the meaning of life, and the meaning about all life in all creation since the beginning. In this book I will have to become the primary actor and subject because it is through my experiences and searching for that "pearl of great price" (Mt 13:44–46) that a drama unfolds and within it, discoveries are made.

In their book *The Grateful Heart*, Wilkie Au and Noreen Cannon provide meaningful nuance for the parable of the merchant's search for fine pearls that entails an active process of searching; the parable of the hidden treasure in the field suggests the person *found or stumbled* onto something very precious, for which he was willing to sell all that he had to possess.[1] Both parables resonate with my story. At times my search was intentional like the merchant's search for fine pearls, and other times I just happened upon the treasure waiting to be found. Along the way these treasures, not so really hidden, became defining discoveries of who I am and also provided direction for my journey, a journey which has an end and final goal.

The experiences which make up this story are myriad and unique to the drama of my life as they are to each and every individual on their own quest for meaning and truth. Mine have taken me down paths of triumph, victory, sorrow, suffering, love and inspiration; in the end, culminating in locating that precious pearl which was partially hidden, throughout my quest along a path of lust for life in the search for purpose and meaning.

We will encounter failure, missteps, challenges overcome, joy, wonder and awe with a glance toward the Director and Creator of this creature on a quest and in search of its purpose. During this journey we will travel through thickets of dark depression and bright life giving, miraculous light

---

[1] See Au, Wilkie and Noreen Cannon Au, *Grateful Heart*, 168–69.

on the precarious search for identity. There are victories and defeats, laughter and tears, joyful encounters, and sorrows. All the stuff which is life . . . and more.

The journey will bring us to the enchanted tropics of Burma (Myanmar) where beauty and a Beauty are found, excursions to meet drug cartel bosses while working undercover as a DEA Special Agent in Peru and Ecuador, and mastering a scheme to ensnare drug trafficking kingpins in Haiti leading to ultimately take down a president and change how US law enforcement operates there. Plenty of adrenalin inducing episodes are part of the scenery along the path, but they were chosen ones, all culminating in a personal discovery of who I really am and for what purpose I was called into being. It is how I was wondrously made for this particular adventure, not yet completed, but modified as time has its own way on characterizing life. Come along on an exciting, wild ride with me in pursuit of that precious pearl.

There are three motivating factors which largely served to inspire me to write this book. The first is my experience with the Drug Enforcement Administration (DEA) and in particular, what evolved into a story worth telling about my experience in Haiti during my nearly five years of working as a Special Agent there. The assignment was to the Port-au-Prince "Country Office." Besides having domestic offices in every large city in the United States, and in many smaller cities as well, the DEA has a presence in many capital cities and other major hubs throughout the world; in Asia, Africa, Europe, South America, Central America, Mexico, Canada, and the Pacific Islands, pretty much covering the globe where people and commerce exist. The DEA has over 70 such offices in foreign countries, some large and some very small, depending on multiple factors. Some offices offer pretty small potential for a lot of excitement and adventure while others can potentially take you on a wild ride, the likes of which you may never see in a lifetime, even in law enforcement. Haiti was the latter for me. The time I spent there, early 1999 to late 2003, came to be for me a "perfect storm" moment in time within the larger context of Haiti's troubled history.

The second factor was the encouragement from a dear friend of my mother who does documentary journalism, to memorialize my experiences there because she had a keen interest in doing a documentary film of some sort, with my collaboration. I did not follow up with her offer but later thought, "well, okay," maybe there is a story worth telling. While you are living out such an experience however, you are just "in the moment," doing what the situation calls for, and it consumes your focus. At the time, never did telling a story cross my mind. But I eventually bought into her idea of documenting the story, at least minimally by jotting down some notes to keep my experience within the reaches of memory, just in case I would later be moved to share it.

When I finished my time in Haiti and with the DEA a few years later, a lifelong friend whom I had known from early adolescence, asked me to speak to a men's group at his church about my "Haiti experience." I agreed to it and fortunately, in preparation for the talk had to rehearse all the events and dynamics which contributed to the experience in my mind, culminating in a written outline, which re-enforced, for the sake of memory, events and individuals who acted them out. Looking back, I do not feel that these two influences were just accidents that happened in some random way, but rather appeared for a reason and higher purpose.

Which leads me to the third motivating influence. I have always been aware, from my earliest days, of the spiritually Divine presence dwelling within, and which is manifest throughout all God's creation, much more than what I can grasp on a sensory and intellectual level. I have always been aware of a movement going on at a deeper level which cannot be adequately described with the mere words of our language, or images for that matter. It is a movement, or stirring deep in the soul. I believe it is a spark of the Divine which resides in us as humans who are created in God's image. I have always been very attracted to this indwelling of the Spirit and have always had an unquenchable desire to share it with others, but to find people open enough to listen to these stirrings and thoughts, and posture themselves as receptive to my expression of them, I've found to be very few. As a result, one learns while going through life that it is best to be guarded about such mystery. That became a learned lesson for me when, with a girl whom I felt I had fallen madly in love with at an early age, while sitting one day on the bank of the Mississippi River watching the river flow southward, and simultaneously marveling at the white puffy clouds flowing northward, I tried to express to her my innermost feelings in that wonderful, magical moment. It was something about feeling God's powerful, all-encompassing love while sitting with her and loving her more because of it, the two forces of love converging into one. Her response to me was that she didn't think she could ever marry me because I loved God too much. So much for sharing intimate inner feelings with someone.

It wasn't until many years later while working on my master's degree in Theology at Loyola Marymount University in Los Angeles, with a focus on the practice of Spiritual Direction with my favorite professor Wilkie Au, did I learn to trust in sharing intimate thoughts and experiences again. There was a deep satisfaction and joy that accompanied the process. I learned to trust in it again. More importantly, the thought occurred to me that perhaps it is my obligation to share thoughts and experiences for the possible benefit of others because of God's love for all his creation and each and every creature in it. God wants to be spread around and shared. Thus, we are created, to do just that.

The fourth motivation, arising out of three, came from my brother, who himself has a book recently published (*Defying Gravity: How Choosing Joy Lifted my Family from Death to Life,* by Joe Sikorra, Ignatius Press). An inspirational book in and of itself, Joe hounded me relentlessly for years to write my story and although I vaguely had a feeling that there might be some merit in doing that, I couldn't work up the right combination of courage, motivation and organization in my mind to actually start. One inspired day I got mad enough at myself for procrastinating and just sat down at the computer and started to write. The following pages are what resulted, for better or worse. The process of writing and completing the project eventually evolved into a joyful endeavor.

PART I

Exploring the Path of Life

1

On your Mark, Get Set, Go!

Running, running, running, back and forth across my parents' yard overlooking the Mississippi River, on a late spring day not too long after I had learned to run, feeling full of life, the power of life, and the joy of life. This may have been my first venture into experiencing God. Although I wouldn't have been able to articulate it as such at the time, I was experiencing life and its Author.

In his book *Toward God, The Ancient Wisdom of Western Prayer*, Michael Casey talks about those people who are seekers, stamped from their earliest years as those in search of the Absolute who can never take the realities of this world as final. That early life experience gives them a certain mold in thinking about themselves and the world; their way is not bound to abstract or theoretical propositions but is intuitive, universal, and unstructured. They may find a faith that embodies, in an approximate way, what they have experienced. Some may succeed in integrating what they have experienced strongly into a personal lifestyle or they may remain always on the fringe, impatient with words or rules that do not mirror what they have "seen." To avoid the pain of being different they may repress their experience and live as though nothing has happened, which is unfortunate and regrettable.[1] I would choose the former and would advise anyone to do the same. These are gifts of grace to give us guidance on life's journey to become complete and whole. We will never be perfect in this world but we would benefit in having that as a goal on our horizon looking forward. I always

---

1. Casey, *Toward God*, 30.

knew that I was far from perfect but knew from that day long ago on the river bank, going forward I would give my best shot at living life in pursuit of finding its meaning and my place within it.

A person on The Way toward the goal that is seeking God, cannot expect continual progress or unfettered determination. We wobble along the journey and stumble off the path at times. We may find ourselves being pulled in other directions by other attractions, stand still or even regress. This is almost universally the natural course. What is significant is the power of the reflex that keeps us bouncing back. Casey says "There is something we keep returning to: a vision, a dream, a hope. Something gives us the courage to get up after each fall and resume the journey. This is concrete evidence of the Spirit's work, far more potent than any spiritual euphoria."[2]

Trial and Errors

After a dazzling high school career, with a track scholarship to the University of Minnesota in hand, the world seemed like a big one, exciting and full of countless possibilities. The security and success of high school was in the past and a vast ocean of the unknown lay ahead of me. I wasn't totally confident about what the future would bring, but dreaming about what it might, was an exciting endeavor to be engaged in. I was bolstered by what I had accomplished in my high school career and at that juncture in my life it gave me confidence to take on the challenges of college. I was excited to walk into the unknown and explore what possibilities lay in wait. I had a fairly sterling running career in high school and had worked very hard at becoming one of the top distance runners in the state of Minnesota. I had my credentials.

When I arrived at the U of M, bliss was hardly my experience. In fact, it wasn't very exhilarating at all, as I was used to being on the top of the hierarchy, but now I was on the bottom looking up at sub four-minute milers, NCAA champions, and Olympians. I felt a little overwhelmed and sensed burn out settling in. The fire I had for my running career was going from wild flames to smoldering cinders. By midyear of my freshman year, I felt my horizons shifting. Being a champion athlete no longer held the same weight nor the anchor for defining who I was or what I was. I began to perceive that there was something much more profound in the "calling" which was stirring within me. I guess you can call this growing, in all its different mysterious forms. I arrived at a decision to give the seminary a try, at the urging of a priest "friend" who in the end turned out not to be a very good friend at all, to see if a vocation to the priesthood was my calling.

2. Casey, *Toward God*, 122–23.

Since I was a child, I had thoughts about it, probably in large part because my Uncle Jack, who I revered, was a priest when I was young and most likely I wanted to emulate him. He later abdicated his vocation which poured some water on my perceived warm stirrings of attraction for that life but I had to try it on nonetheless, just to see if it was the right fit. My Uncle Jack had from early childhood ignited a spark of attractiveness for just living in me that I was dramatically drawn to in my early developmental years. During my discernment about a vocation later, I associated the youthful attractive spark with some kind of possible calling to the priesthood. Reflection upon that motivational influence now, I would admit that it was more than the illusory attractiveness projected by my uncle. I needed some kind of "noble" reason to justify my disenchantment and abdication of my running career and the full scholarship to the U of M that I was throwing away. I had to save face, at least in my juvenile way of thinking at the time. I felt transitioning to the seminary was the higher road and a neat justification to resolve that ghost of a dilemma. I needed to find footing on an increasingly slippery road.

Putting my running career on hold, I transferred to the University of St. Thomas in St. Paul, Minnesota and entered the seminary of St. John Vianney. I also joined a Chamber singing group to provide some nourishment for my musical and theatrical cravings. I felt reasonably comfortable in my new trajectory of culture and vocation. Music and drama were not foreign to my upbringing. I had studied the violin since the second grade and had also been part of my high school's choir, while participating in a musical or two. I was happy in my new environment and made new friends at school and in the seminary.

The priest "friend," who really wasn't, as I learned far too late in our relationship, was radically disordered, and also radically deceitful. His years of pretending to be a mentor and friend turned out to be a horribly misdirected subterfuge to try to do to me what many priests over the years have done to countless victims. What I experienced was unfortunately part of the distorted and sad history of scandal within the Church where hundreds of boys were sexually exploited and abused by priests. But fortunate for me, I was mature enough by the time he attempted to make me a victim, that I had the where-with-all to repel his unwanted advance, despite his unheroic tactic of attempting to distort my judgement and will with copious amounts of alcohol, at least amounts that I was not used to. The psychological wound that his deceit inflicted, however, should not be ignored, I would later come to realize. To have been set up and taken advantage of was a traumatic awakening. The trauma that wasn't really that traumatic in the end probably was more a feeling of shame for having allowed myself to be duped into that sort of sick scenario. I accepted the dinners at restaurants and the gifts of cigarettes which he got me hooked on. I felt guilt for falling into his trap but more so, the shattering of trust in relationships leaves scars on the psyche and the soul. These are the treacherous potholes of human interaction and relationships. I learned from that experience, which was far from the *authentic* I was seeking. "Move on" was my self-imposed directive.

Before the violation of my personal orientation and assault on my dignity I hadn't become convinced that the priesthood was part of my overarching career path, but at least I had done due diligence in testing the waters. I had a clear conscience upon leaving the seminary. I had come to the realization that a life commitment to that particular vocation didn't seem to be the right fit. Abandoning that career path was a matter of judgement that involved taking an honest look at who I really was. I didn't find the *authentic* in that system either. I can't say that I was influenced by any particular person or event in arriving at that decision. Not over thinking it, I simply came to the conclusion that it just wasn't me.

But I was having a good time with the musical group, rehearsing daily and doing musical performances with the Chamber Singers. It was a fun group to be involved with. It was small and had a rather elite status on campus due to its reputation and professional like image. I didn't realize it at the time but being so wrapped up in the image of the group was almost too inward looking. There was a world outside the Chamber Singers but I wasn't noticing it at the time. The group and its identity were engaging, fun, yet a bit consuming, but filled a need at the time, however the mirage it really was.

As I reflect back on the situation with the singing group, I see living in that small world a bit like life in a cocoon, not necessarily healthy in terms of general development and preparation for adulthood and the accompanying trials that the sometimes-harsh world presents. It wasn't until after college and working in the real world, for survival and striving for adult dreams of a different nature, that I realized my fantasy world of singing and performing were wholly secondary to what the world and adulthood demanded. We did, however, carry on for a bit after graduation with a smaller core group doing church music and singing carols at Christmas, but that too eventually faded with the larger realities of life descending.

Music and Social Dynamics, an off-Key Tune

The chamber group was managed and directed by a sister of the St. Joseph Order who we referred to as "The Nun." What now, in retrospect, seems a bit odd was all the parring up of couples within the group which led to numerous marriages among the group's members. Back then it seemed quite cool and the right thing to strive for. In fact, I think there were couples and marriages within the group involving most every person except one guy who became a priest and later bishop, eventually being elevated to Cardinal. Blasé was a very focused person, unlike me. I eventually fell into the trap of this "group dynamic," which at the time just seemed like the normal way to go about life. This undiscerned social anomaly would later turn into a disaster, and not just for me. I get it that there is a certain attraction for couples to come together with common interests and the attractive lure of music enhancing the attraction even more so, but with this particular group that phenomenon seems to me now a little over the top. Was the Nun somehow encouraging this intergroup coupling? A fair question to ask.

As the years passed by, however, many of those marriages did not survive. Some did. At the time though, there was a strong attraction and pull toward that unique group identity ultimately resulting in marriages of couples from within the group. Maybe it was the attraction of being able to identify with something and people who all enjoyed making music together. At the time it was intoxicating and I drank of the nectar. I would later come to realize that I was not being true to my authentic self. It was a compelling dynamic at the time, though. It was the irresistible lure of this group identity that overshadowed and clouded what should have been the ongoing development as an adolescent moving toward young adulthood. The attraction of this group thing temporarily derailed my center of gravity and judgement. It put me on the wrong path and would later have deleterious implications for my life. We impulsively step into pot holes that we blindly encounter, not having yet discovered our authentic selves through experience and growth. But then human development often demands that we stumble and fall, especially when young and inexperienced.

2

Becoming by Failing

That we stumble and fall to temptations in the way of sin is part of our human nature. Growing in our development emotionally, psychologically, and spiritually is by becoming aware of the reality of our shortcomings and sin in our life. This causes grief because delusions and complacency will be shattered. Becoming whole or complete requires a lifetime of repairing damage and avoiding future harm, only with the help and aid of grace. Julian of Norwich provides her thought on this poignant teaching:

> After this [God] allows us to fall harder and more grievously than ever we did before—as it seems to us. And then we think (because we are not all wise) that what we had begun has come to nothing. But it is not so. It is necessary for us to fall and it is necessary for us to see it. For if we did not fall, we should not know how feeble and wretched we are on our own, nor should we know so fully the marvelous love of our Maker. For in truth, we shall see in heaven, for all eternity that though we have grievously sinned in life, we were never hurt in God's love, nor were we ever of less value in God's sight. This falling is a test by which we shall have a high and marvelous knowing of love in God forever. That love is hard and marvelous that cannot and will not be broken for [our] trespasses. [1]

By our falling and seeing it as it is, that we are needy and weak, we give ourselves a chance to see the mysteries of divine mercy and grace.

---

1. Casey, *Toward God*, 151.

During the summer after my freshman year at the University of St. Thomas my family moved from our home on the Mississippi River in Minnesota to Florida, where my dad, an aerospace engineer at Honeywell, was transferred to. I accompanied my family on the move to Florida in early June and during the summer I worked at a chemical plant in Tarpon Springs while staying with my parents and younger siblings.

I returned to St. Thomas and the seminary in the fall but only a couple months into the semester a friend and fellow seminarian and I decided that we both had given the situation a fair shot and we conspired to leave our seminary life, break out on our own together and find a place to live. My co-conspirator, Larry, in "the escape" didn't influence me, nor I him but we were a support for one another as we ventured out of the cocoon. It was another significant life event and it was comforting to have a friend to share the eventful change in life direction with.

We found a rather dumpy but cheap place to rent a couple miles from the University and re-joined the secular world. I was really in no financial position to go out on my own as I had no income and really can't say how I managed to make my contribution to the monthly rent obligations let alone buy groceries. My quality of life and health started to deteriorate both physically, from poor nutrition and consequently, mentally as well. I did not have an adequate support system in place to maintain a healthy footing and began to spiral in the wrong direction from up. I guess I had been a little too impulsive with my life decisions. Nothing new here. Recklessness must be a requisite for the young, at least it was my modus operandi in the early days. Depression and anxiety began to creep in as I was careening toward a life changing experience while being caught in the jaws of a steep and rapid descent into darkening territory that I could not seem to apply the brakes to, as hard as I pressed on them.

Descent into Darkness

The blackness swooped in like a spring thunderstorm in the Midwest. Depression and anxiety took a death grip on my entire being, crippling my ability to function adequately, or at all for that matter. I found myself hardly able to move, alarming my two roommates, one of whom was studying psychology. Jay and Larry arranged to have me hospitalized and I found myself in the psych ward at St. Joseph's Hospital, in Saint Paul. I hardly realized what was happening and placidly forfeited my depleted will to their game plan. I had not the wherewithal to resist and I knew clearly that I needed help, badly. All I knew with certainty was that I needed relief from the debilitating anxiety and blackness which had engulfed me. At the hospital I was barely cognizant of my environment or the people around me, possibly from medication the hospital staff may have administered to me. I had some sessions with a psychologist but don't recall any revelations coming from the encounters. I was released after about a week but felt a long way from being well. Acute depression is a sinister monster which can feel like living death, worse than that of real death because you are still feeling. I muddled along, functioning as best I could, probably with the aid of medications, although I don't remember.

I can't say why or how this happened so suddenly and severely. Humans, while capable of great and noble acts and story book heroics are very fragile creatures at the same time. The doctor with whom I consulted explained the situation as being situational in nature. It came about because of my rather bleak conditions. I had made some bad calculations as they related to reality and without my dad's support or endorsement of my continuing future plans for my college career, I was left to fend for myself. Should I have sought a job to support my endeavors? Yes, but I had no transportation and was still clinging to my Chamber Singers fantasy. I was a reed blowing in the wind, still living in a dream world in contradiction to one set in reality. This is a recipe for disaster which made its introduction forcefully in the form of deadly depression and anxiety. A rather dramatic corrective measure, but it did its corrective work in the end.

I recall one late March evening scrounging up enough change to purchase a beer at the local Irish pub on Snelling Avenue which was within walking distance of where I was temporarily staying. I needed to contemplate my situation in a different environment for a few divergent minutes. I drank my beer wondering what this foreign, unwanted state of affairs all meant but came to no specific conclusion. Upon exiting the pub, I embarked on voyaging across the four-lane street thinking it would be just fine if I were hit by a car to allow me to separate myself from that dreadful, dark state of existence. It wasn't a suicide contemplation, just a fantasy about escaping the smothering, heavy blackness. I'm not sure if I even checked for oncoming traffic, even though it was a fairly well travelled four lane city street. I probably did because I was taught at an early age to do so.

The Rescue, Resurrection and Free Ride Across the Street

An amazing thing happened when I had traversed roughly half the wide street. I suddenly found myself looking down from above at myself in the middle of Snelling Avenue, in Saint Paul, Minnesota. There was a presence on my right side as I hovered above my body and a voice said: "Look at him, I love him very much and I will take care of him."

The next thing I knew, I was back in my physical body on the other side of the street thinking: What just happened? I felt a little shocked and giddy at the same time and it occurred to me that I would find my way out of this darkness with some very much appreciated, grace gifted help that I suddenly and profoundly felt with a grounded certainty in the mystical reality of "resurrection" life. I could and would continue going forward. I was awash in gratefulness, with light flowing into my consciousness and senses. Grace often comes gift wrapped in the darkness of trials and suffering.

Back at the house of a friend where I was temporarily staying, I prepared for sleep where I had a cot in the basement. Suddenly there was a palpable warm light that flooded the room and engulfed me. There were no words but it pulsed joy into the room and into my conscious being. I hadn't felt joy in months and I just gazed at the warm, loving light which was at the same time powerful and reassuring, offering me a sober and powerful sense of providential contentment. All would be well, I strongly sensed in that life-transcending moment. I was not alone, I knew, and would survive with the help of this visiting Spirit Helper.

Be still in God's light as he communicates Love to you. There is no force in the universe as powerful as his love which has no limit. It fills all of space, time and eternity. Our vision is clouded now but someday we will see him face to face and will experience fully how wide and long and deep is his love.

> For God, who said, "Let light shine out of darkness," made His light shine in our hearts to give us the light of the knowledge of the glory of God in the face of Christ, -2 Corinthians 4:6
> And so, we have the prophetic word confirmed, which you do well to heed as a light that shines in a dark place, until the day dawns and the morning star rises in your hearts. -2 Peter 1:19.

The following day the residue of that joy from the night before remained with me and I made an affirmation that this process of healing from the depths of depression would require taking one step at a time and trusting in that process. It took time to fight off the anxiety but step by step I left it behind. I was ready to start living life again. I received a lot of understanding from my teachers and professors and managed to successfully complete my sophomore spring semester. Above all, it was grace that saved me and pulled me up from and out of the mud and mire that had taken control of my being. The lifesaving vision in the basement of that house was one of beautiful beaming rays of grace in an array of heavenly colors on the brighter side of the rainbow.

In Casey's *Toward God,* he states that he has never come across a man, woman or child who has not experienced suffering. After the trauma of birth, we pass through many difficulties and hurtful encounters before that dreaded moment of death. We may have public or private tragedies, sufferings and anxieties along with our own deep, unspoken fears. This is the stuff of human life. It is precisely the depths of our sense of pain and suffering that marks us as human. Yet in the very worst moment of our suffering, Casey goes on to say, often a spark of life appears. "When all appears dead and wintery, a sign of spring is shown us—all the more real and profoundly experienced because we have seen the worst."[2]

In tales written about the Buddha, before becoming Buddha, Siddhartha, the Prince, in his attempt to find the remedy to suffering and death went through several stages of exploration in Eastern religious traditions. These included extreme asceticism, depriving his body of nutrients or any bodily sustenance, out doing all of his fellow ascetics in his herculean efforts. On the brink of death, in his memory he returned to a moment in his youth where he remembered his step mother giving him a bowl of rice pudding. At that moment a young girl, seeing his emaciated, starving body, offered him the same, which he took and ate. Siddhartha, in that moment realized that suffering was integral to human life and not something to escape from. But rather, enlightenment which he was seeking must come from within, and vividly had a vision of how all creation is connected. He abandoned his extreme ascetic practice to the chagrin of his co-practitioners and then looking within himself made a choice to embrace everything, including suffering, along with joy and contentment.

In his book *The Developing Christian: Spiritual Growth through the Life Cycle,* Peter Feldmeier says that the first and most important expression of the earliest stages of young adulthood is the process of leaving home. It can be the most exciting, anticipated, desired and ambivalent period in a young adult's life. It was rather not so much a choice in my case as it was force fed to me when my dad was transferred to Saint Petersburg, Florida with Honeywell's Aerospace Division. I could have stayed connected to my family and moved with them to Florida and attended school there, which my dad strongly advised. But I chose the rebellious route of non-planned independence, for other reasons—the enchanting attractions of romance and music. I had launched myself onto my self-designed unsecured course of travel into young adult life and was hell bent on making it work, ill-advised, as the lack

---

2. Casey, *Toward God,* 5–6.

of having a solid plan was. I did meet with hell briefly, but then experienced resurrection.

Feldmeier explains further that this is a precarious period for the young adult, on a scale at a minimum of high vulnerability up to depression. (Bingo, I hit the Jack Pot!) One has to deal with the grief of the loss of one's home base while not yet feeling at home in the world, Feldmeier states. It is a move from the embeddedness of the family toward self-authorship and psychological autonomy. More than just leaving home, the young adult is reconstructing a new relationship with him/herself and with others.[3] Additionally, tendencies of my own doing, inclined toward folly through impulsive, and not well thought through decisions in my search for self-identity and independence have to be factored into the larger equation. My dad had offered prudent advice about going to school in Florida and living at home. That was recklessly not for me.

Feldmeier also posits that two of the greatest concerns for all humans are identity and belonging, and further that they are inseparable, but for most, one only can achieve real identity by cultivating one's own self-definition. Experimenting with trying on *roles* for size is part of the process of defining one's self and it is a dominant psychological theme during post high school years, particularly in the college environment. It is easy for the young adult to slip into roles that seem to be expected of them without correlating these with their truest sense of self. That was most certainly evident in my case. I was searching and fighting for my own identity by becoming independent while falling into unseen traps of exterior persuasive attractions. One great aspect that life sometimes graciously offers is an opportunity to correct mistakes made, "a second chance."[4]

---

3. Feldmeier, *Developing Christian*, 129.
4. Feldmeier, *Developing Christian*, 134–36.

3

Belonging with an Identify Built on Dust

Having briefly discussed the Chamber Singers unique social phenomenon earlier, I failed to address my personal role playing out in that drama. I fell into the trap of infatuation with a young lady in the singing group who had quite a spectacular singing voice and who was one year my senior in school. The power of wanting to have an identity with "the group" and "belong" seemed to draw me into the pursuit of a relationship with her that later would prove to be life changing, taking me down a road that I would later come to regret. But whisked up in the current of things I strapped on the identity of the group by finding a partner and claimed that identity as my own. This was another wrong turn, but who knows? Sometimes wrong turns get us to the right place with just a little extra unexpected scenery along the path.

In my sophomore year during the semester break, before things totally crumbled around me, our chamber group did a singing tour in Europe, performing in Germany, Austria and Italy. I don't have a very vivid recollection of the details because already, the oncoming onslaught of depression was beginning to affect my perception of things going on in my world. It was all kind of a blur, but it was also in this dimly lit perception of reality and declining mental state that the girl with the angelic voice and I agreed that we should get married. Not really a proposal on which to find footing, because I was in no any way near in possession of anything approximating lucid clarity of mind to make such a life impacting decision. But there I was, diving off a cliff in Europe to guarantee, solidify, and satisfy group identification. Everyone else was getting married or planning to do so and I just went with the flow, thinking (or not) for the sake of my newly acquired fragile identity, that it was the right thing to do. Years later this would be the foundational argument for my annulment, the "fatal flaw," in legal terms, right from the beginning, was that I was not thinking clearly at all, and was fast cruising toward the psych ward at St. Joseph Hospital.

During the summer after my tumultuous sophomore year, I again returned to Florida and took a job for the few weeks I had there. My Dad's efforts trying to convince me to stay and attend the University of Central Florida in Tampa were in vain. I would have none of that. I explained that I was in a "serious" relationship and had to return to St. Paul. There was no convincing me but it was pretty clear going forward, I was on my own with no additional support coming from him. Fair enough. I get that now and got it then, that he did not agree with my folly, but I needed my freedom. I returned in the fall and moved back into our dumpy but adequate rental house in St. Paul, with my old roommates.

My now ex-wife would be graduating from the College of Saint Catherine at the end of the fall semester, and although not studying specifically for a major in music, it was her area of specialty within her Elementary Education Degree, as a music teacher. Therefore, she was required to prepare for and perform a "senior recital." She had an amazing operatic soprano voice which I clearly see now, was what I was in love with, more than the person who she was. Although she is a fine person, that wasn't the strong pull of my attraction. It was infatuation with her and being in love with her voice! I was, however, very proud of her accomplishments and communicated that enthusiasm to my parents and family. The day before the recital I was very much surprised by an unannounced visit by my mom and her brother Jack, who was one of my most beloved persons on the planet. A surprise visit, all the way from Florida to honor my soon to be wife, whom she had yet to meet. The encounter would be on terms that would certainly make a lasting first impression with a dynamic, stirring, and powerful performance! It was also a show of support for me, I suppose. These were all false assumptions about reality though. It was really more about pretty sounds and pretenses. It was a play on a stage with constructed sets and leading roles dressed up in attractive costumes. The performance was superb and I was filled with pride, which can be a misleading and even deceitful emotion that masks truth. Nonetheless, it was a great introduction of her to some of my family and indeed, a dramatic one in my mind.

Emerging from the Dark, in Pre-Dawn Light

Buoyed by making plans to get married the following summer and feeling somewhat like an adult and independent, my junior year in college went somewhat smoother than the previous one. I got a part time job at JC Penney's and had a little income coming in which made life, financially, a little more manageable. The wedding was being planned for June after the school year. I would have barely turned 21 years old by then and I felt emboldened to be a "legal" adult. My soon to be bride would be graduating with a teaching degree in December and would already have found a teaching job before her graduation. Things were falling into place nicely. With God's grace I was becoming whole once again and while not all the way back, I felt human enough again to recognize I was alive and could once again see beauty in the world around me.

I was saddened however, one day by the news that a former member of the Chamber Singers had taken his own life by jumping off the Mississippi River bridge into the river below, where it connects Saint Paul with Minneapolis. Stevie was very much undersized and really struggled socially, although a very bright individual. He was an awkward person and his involvement with the Chamber Singers was probably a good thing for him to help with his social awkwardness and self-esteem. It obviously didn't quite do enough for him though.

As was typical of him, upon our arrival in Luxemburg for our singing tour in Europe, he and everyone else were chagrinned to find out he didn't have his passport, whether it was lost or forgotten by him I'm not sure. It upset everyone because there was a big delay in keeping to our itinerary, but frankly it surprised no one either. Just characteristic Stevie. The news of his self-inflicted death left me feeling pain for him, that he carried so much of it within himself, ultimately moving him to take his own life. That is the pinnacle of despair and sadly, usually goes unnoticed. Had I or anyone seen that he was in such pain, I would have wanted to try to reach him and talk to him about it. I had done so with a childhood family friend, years earlier when we were just kids.

My friend was staying with our family for the summer during a time when he was lost and experiencing awkwardness in his own life. His parents thought that it would be good for him to spend some time with my large family dominated by boys and take a break from his large family that was dominated by girls. I just remember talking to him about how much God loved him and cherished him just for being who he was. It wasn't until many years later when we were well into adulthood that he communicated to me indirectly that I had had a profound impact on his life, from that moment years earlier, while quietly talking to him in one of the multiple upstairs bedrooms of our home. We never know how far a small kindness can influence someone and redirect a life. It's a power wrapped in mystery.

A Botched High Dive into Troubled Waters

Toward the end of June, after my junior year, my singing companions from the Chamber Singers drove to Upstate New York to provide music for the wedding. My family drove up from Florida and a dear priest friend came from Minnesota to marry us in a little country church, about the size of a large living room, just outside Auburn, New York. Decorations for the event were provided by the efforts of family and guests who had picked colorful wild flowers from my bride's parent's 10-acre former family farm turned natural. The night before the wedding I felt much trepidation about what was to take place the following day, but I was in a jam after all the commitment, time and expense that everyone in attendance had incurred to get there, so kept my feelings to myself. I was developing a bad habit of making life changing blunders and I was just barely 21 years old. The wedding itself was a hoot as was the outdoor reception party in the large manicured yard tucked in near to the house on the edge of the former farm.

Our plan was to drive to Florida after the wedding where I would find a job for the summer. The first night of my new life was spent at a Holiday Inn near Syracuse, NY. An acute sense of loneliness swept over me as we settled into the room. Maybe the reason was because we just left the company of partying family and friends and were now alone just by ourselves, or maybe it was something deeper. Gone, at least temporarily, was the social identity and persuasion of the "group" dynamic. It was replaced by an awareness of the reality that it was now about me and my new bride. The realization that I now had an obligation to abruptly grow out of the cocoon of the group and as a couple declare a certain independence with a new identity and vision swept over me. I was not looking forward to the future all of a sudden. After the first night, it was a straight through drive to Clearwater, FL where we rented a small apartment for the summer. I landed a job with a dairy distributor and drove a milk delivery route up and down the Gulf Coast north of Clearwater for the next five or six weeks. Late in the summer we returned to St. Paul and found an apartment within walking distance of my school. My new wife returned to her teaching job. It was a comfort not having to worry about starving and how to pay rent, and good to just focus on finishing my degree and graduate the following Spring. During the year we concentrated on trying to save enough money for a down payment to buy a small townhouse closer to her job following my graduation, on the solid advice of my wife's cousin, a realtor.

The following year was smooth but frugal. My goal of graduation within reach in the Spring, along with a warming sun and new Springtime life coming into view all around, I graduated with an accompanying sense of accomplishment and a new set of goals set out before me. There was a fresh scent of optimism in the air.

4

Growing Pains and Growing Up

I had always tended toward the reckless side of caution and would seek adventure over safety and prudence, which most often, locates trouble. Davy Crockett, the Swamp Fox, Zorro and the Lone Ranger were my childhood heroes and role models. So, I've dated myself, but they were alive in my world and available to inspire and give energy to my imagination then.

On one of my birthdays, somewhere in the six- or seven-year range, I received as a gift what I dearly wished for, a buck skin jacket with fringe on the sleeves and chest. This was inspired by Davey Crockett of course, and made me feel all the more invincible. One day, donning my newly acquired prized apparel, my friends and I (imagined or real, I don't recall) went out to play some sort of imaginary battle game. I climbed atop an outdoor brick fire pit with a grill set in it. The top of the structure was five or six feet tall and while trying to balance on the top of it declaring victory in the make-believe battle, I fell head first onto the grill causing a huge gash to the left side of my head very near the temple area. I bled profusely, and while my mom did yet another emergency run to the doctor, I proceeded to soak my cherished leather jacket with the fringes in blood. When it dried it stiffened and was badly discolored, totally in disharmony with the rest of the soft leather. I lived to write about it now, although the doctor said one quarter inch closer to the temple and I wouldn't have. I cried more for my jacket than my injury. My mom salvaged most of the disfigured jacket but had to cut out two large panels on the front of it and replace the leather cut-outs with some plaid patterned fabric far inferior to the soft yet empowering feel of buck skin leather. I never wore it with the same pride or joy again. It looked very unlike Davey Crockett and wearing it post injury just brought on feelings of sadness and defeat despite my proud declaration of victory atop the fire pit "mountain."

Big Island Tales

A few years later we were vacationing on "Big Island," a former war veteran's R & R center turned civilian vacation resort after WW II, on Lake Minnetonka just west of Minneapolis. It was a wonderful place to vacation with a family, there being plenty of water and other activities. With eight kids in our family, it was an affordable vacation destination for my parents and their tribe with plenty of space to roam about safely. It was a fun place to vacation because there were also many other families with kids our age who most always planned to spend the same week there every year. We made fast friends with people whom we were sure to see for one or two weeks every year.

One summer I was at the stage of development where the urge to show off machismo was emerging. I climbed to the top of a pylon at the end of the pier on the beach which jutted straight out into the lake. I intended to make a graceful dive into the water to show off, for whoever might be watching. Instead of pulling off the spectacular event, I slipped, fell, and hit my head on the dock before splashing into the lake and sinking to the bottom, half conscious. A friend, Danny, pulled me up and out of the Lake Minnetonka depths, which occasionally took a life, and he probably saved mine. The last time I saw him a year or two later, I was staring down into a coffin at his dead body with a repaired bullet hole in the center of his forehead. The vague word out there was that he and a friend had been playing with a gun and something terrible happened, somehow. Maybe the precarious game "Russian Roulette" was popular with him and his buddy. Knowing Danny, the little I did, he would have been a candidate to take that game on thinking it was fun.

Another Big Island story from the same era developed on our makeshift baseball diamond near the main lodge. An unfamiliar person about my age was occupying my position at second base when I showed up for the game. There was a new family on the island that year. Who did he think he was? This was my territory and he was not going to displace me from the position that was my rightful and traditional place. I confronted him about his interloping on my space and my base, and we had some words. I was prepared to fight if it came to that. Then a strange thing happened. We ended up hammering out some kind of compromise (I don't recall what the details actually were) and by game's end we were fast friends. Our relationship grew into a very close friendship before long and it remained so for years. As it turned out, he was being groomed for the Olympics as a ski jumper. We shared similar passions for winter sports. I was a speed skater in my younger years. Jeff came close to his dream being fulfilled. He was on the Junior Olympic Team and was the recipient of professional training and coaching.

It was during my sophomore year in college that I received a phone call and was informed that Jeff had tragically and suddenly died. It was a freak ski jumping accident. His dad told me at Jeff's wake that he made a normal jump, landed well and then just fell over while displaying his style points at the end of his run. I would miss him and I grieved over my loss, his dad's loss and Jeff's lost dream, although now I have no doubt that he is in a much more wonderful winter wonder land with God, probably making spectacular flying jumps. I was beginning to understand that life can be unpredictable, frightening, and yet full of wonder all at the same time.

Crazy Encounters with Brother Pat

The wild tendency in me wasn't left behind in childhood or adolescence but continued into adulthood and was always particularity ignited when I encountered my brother Pat, the horse and equestrian trainer who runs his boarding and teaching operation on the outskirts of Tampa, Florida. The place always struck me as a serene, rural, haven which was nice to visit, even though Pat was far from serene. When we were kids growing up on the Mississippi River, I liked constructing unsophisticated tent structures in a thicket of trees where I could hide out and dream dreams of saints and famous athletes who conquered the unthinkable, while reading books written about them. Pat, in the meantime, would be busy down by the river constructing his boat which he had aspirations of putting a motor on and setting off on his fantasy journey down the river. He completed his project while I contemplated life's meaning. He launched his boat equipped with an outboard motor he had somehow acquired one summer day and proceeded to sink it in the middle of the Mississippi, motor and all. He learned, however, from his failure, through hard work and dreams of his own, with a passion for horses found success in his dream vocation later in life.

The wildness that we brought out in each other is a bit hard to explain. A synergy or energy that was always delightful, but sometimes accompanied by unwanted consequences. Our encounters in adult life were infrequent. He was inexorably tied down by his farm obligations of boarding horses, training them as well as his students, and doing maintenance on the property. I was off working in my own profession in other parts of the country or planet. Most of our visits took place in Florida, my family's home base now, because his obligations tied him down to the farm. One such visit took place when I was visiting my mom at her house in the Clearwater area. I had come from where ever I was stationed at the time. Pat came to welcome me in his normal explosive fashion. Rather than a hug or a hand shake, our greetings always seemed to involve a wrestling scuffle of sorts, but a joyful one that included copious amounts of his rich, deep laughter, so very contagious it was. Our greeting that particular day concluded with me launching him onto the hood of his newly purchased Toyota Camry and smashing in the hood. Typically, expressive and joyful, this time a very expensive greeting of brotherly love.

Another crazy get-together with Pat, among many crazy ones, occurred when I was visiting Florida in the winter. My daughter, having come from Seattle, and I drove out to his farm for dinner and to spend the night. That evening Pat wanted to take me for a ride around his property on his newly purchased 4-wheeler, a perfect way to get around his 10-acre piece of real estate. I hopped on the back, seating myself on a sort of flat metal rack for carrying things, not necessarily people, lacking any sort of cushion for human accommodation of the back side.

We took off in the dark with a singular head lamp minimally illuminating our path. Pat always feeling the need to push things to their limit did not hold back on the throttle, so we raced through his fields in the dark, hitting every bump with jarring force, not doing my behind or tailbone any favors, until the climax of the thrill ride, when it came to an abrupt halt. He forgot about the half-buried cement culvert along one of the paths he chose to navigate. Travelling a bit too fast for the terrain, blindly, we hit the rounded object which propelled us and the machine into the air. I think we both did a flip because we found ourselves lying side by side on our backs staring up at the headlight shining down on us.

The machine had been air born and was falling on a direct path toward us, and fast approaching. It was descending back to earth with the two of us in between the ground and the mass of metal and wheels on a trajectory to land directly upon us. Everything seemed to be happening in slow motion. I threw up my right leg and with my foot I thrust the deadly object off to our right. To my senses it felt as light as a feather. After we lay there for a minute or so wondering why we hadn't been crushed, we painfully worked our way back to our feet. Pat, the grateful witness, will willingly testify that I did in fact toss the threatening machine off to the side, most likely saving our lives.

My daughter who was standing outside on the porch not too far off, saw the whole affair. I could only reason that it was my guardian angel doing an angel's job coming to the rescue, or that I had in that moment acquired some kind of super human strength, which is doubtful. I'm not sure what Pat's theory is, but I reasoned that God wanted us both alive for some reason, at least for the time being. I broke my wrist in the course of our excursion. What was exponentially more painful, however, was my bruised behind and tail bone from the violent bumpy ride while sitting on that metal rack. Thankfully I had my daughter there to drive us home the next morning because there was no way I could have sat behind the steering wheel navigating the 45-minute-long drive back. When we arrived back at my mom's I proceeded to the orthopedic clinic, got an x-ray and had a cast put on my right wrist, negating the golf game I had planned with my friend Jim.

The reason I consider these stories as relevant is more than just their entertainment value. But on a deeper level, I question and wonder at the dynamics of human relational nature and how various personalities interact and evoke different behaviors in one another. Mixing combinations of personalities and how that influences behavior is a psychological intrigue to me. You have heard it said that "he or she brings out the best in me," or "the worst in me," or the "wild" in me.

As I reflect on this propensity for the "wild" that both my brother and I seemed to be drawn toward, I see now as largely the peculiar personality trait that fueled the engine of my eventual desire to seek a career in law enforcement. It would have been a violation of the natural order to suppress that attraction.

5

Prison and the Pursuit of a Dream

John Eldridge says in his book "Wild at Heart" there are three desires which are innate in every male person and etched so deeply into his own heart that if he were to disregard them, he would lose his soul. These three desires are: a battle to fight, an adventure to live, and a beauty to rescue. He is convinced that these three indelible desires placed into the heart of every man, have often been misplaced, forgotten or misdirected. Although part of a man's DNA, he may simply not recognize his true nature or his soul, and therefore never live out his real desires. As the playwright Christopher Fry says,

Life is a hypocrite if I can't live the way it moves me! [1]

I had grown into adulthood, after some false starts, misdirection and potential dead ends, primed to go out into the world to fight my battle and live my adventure. I'd have to put off rescuing a beauty for some time.

During my final year in college at St. Thomas, I befriended a classmate who had returned to school to seek a degree while in his middle thirties. He was a police officer and besides attending college full time, he held down his full-time job as a lieutenant on the Bloomington, Minnesota Police Department. Ken became somewhat of a mentor to me and it was during my final year in school that, partly due to his influence, my aspiration to go into law enforcement as a career came into focus. I also knew others in the profession and looked to them for their input also. There were no ready-made jobs available to me right away so I went to work as a Corrections Officer

---

1. Eldredge, *Wild at Heart*, 9.

at the Minnesota State Prison in Stillwater, Minnesota. My newly acquired friends in the prison would be murderers, robbers, burglars, and various other flavors of criminal persuasion. The experience was both educational and sobering. I recall occasionally seeing a sheet covered body of some poor inmate being rolled out of the institution on a gurney. Sometimes it was a suicide, or more sinister, in that sometimes-hostile environment, a homicide. The prison environment could be a dark and depressing place to live, and work, but for the most part for those whose world it had become, it was a routine that had evolved into a conditioned institutional way of being, albeit in a very restrictive environment.

There was an intriguing array of personalities and a wide range of mood that I encountered among the prison population, including some mentally deranged individuals. A prevailing constant among the inmates was gaming the prison staff in their attempts to solicit favors that would potentially put staff in compromised positions. Simple, innocent requests at first could quickly evolve into more serious matters if not checked at the door. Correction Officers have to maintain a rigid code of behavior if they are to themselves survive the system and stay on the right side of the law.

Motivations for trying to con the guards and other employees was a bit multi-layered. If an inmate could persuade you to smuggle something innocuous into the prison for him it would snowball into more serious things and he would have you caught up in his snare of a sinister strangle hold. Once caught in that snare he could yield his power of compromise and control with blackmail, emphasis on the black aspect. The small favors would balloon into serious contraband because they already had created their leverage with the small, innocent items. Of course, it was a serious offense to smuggle anything into the prison, be it a bag of potato chips to drugs or weapons. It didn't matter what the contraband was, you were in deep trouble bringing anything in for them. Constant self-vigilance was the only rule to follow because the pressure was incessantly present.

Personalities among the inmates were as varied as they are in the outside world. There is no stereotype. There were affable types, and somber, serious ones that you'd be best advised to keep a wary eye on lest they try to harm or even kill you. I can imagine the pressure cooker they live in and it can easily boil over into violence. I saw corrections officers assaulted and stabbed. Among the inmate population there were jokers, slick con men, some pleasant characters who had found religion and those who you just sensed were very bad people and best stay clear of. It was an intriguing, colorful world (on the darker side of the spectrum) to experience, although one I didn't want to necessarily make a career of. I went from being a guard to a case-worker to the Resident Parole Agent and coordinator for the Parole

Board all in the short span of three years. I could have made a career there but my dream was to be a cop. I didn't want to just be a guardian of the robbers, I wanted to play *Cops and Robbers.*

Wakening to A Dream

All the while in prison, for eight hours a day, I made applications to numerous police agencies within the Minneapolis, Saint Paul area when vacancy announcements were posted. There weren't many. It was frustrating because I was restrained from expanding my geographic pursuit to areas outside the state because of my wife's teaching career. I was also fighting against what was a nationwide policy of "absolute veteran's preference" at the time and took my place in line behind the veterans, mostly from the Vietnam war. I was used to finding success in most all of my quests in life up to this point and had not yet been sufficiently conditioned or trained for the vitally important virtue and requirement in life, patience. I had to learn the golden art and precious practice of patience in order to dance with any sort of grace in this exacting and linear world in which we live. I wanted instant success in my professional pursuit of becoming a cop, but I needed to learn the lesson of how grace works through patience with trust.

The frustration with rejection boiled over one day after a non-response from yet another attempt to land the "right" job and found myself, once again, on the banks of the Mississippi River, this time in Saint Paul, Minnesota, adjacent to the Saint John Vianney Seminary Dormitory, where I had lived for nearly a year. Sitting on a large boulder on the cliff overlooking the river flowing downstream, the piercing pain of youthful frustration overwhelmed me. The lazily flowing water on its natural flow downstream brought tears to my eyes, joining with the river in its mighty flow of water to the South. There I prayed and there I was gifted with a stream of grace. Patience my child, patience.

Finally, one day, I received a letter from a Minneapolis suburban department inviting me for an interview after having taken numerous written tests. The interview went very well. You just seem to know when you are clicking with the people with whom you are engaged in certain situations. There was a positive vibe in the room. It was an early summer, sunny evening and the drive home from that encounter was accompanied by a solid sense of satisfaction filling my entire being. Following the interview was a physical agility test and an agonizing waiting period that seemed to stretch on for an eternity. I was receiving positive sounding signals from the police chief's secretary and then one magical day a letter from the city arrived in the mail box. I was being offered a job as a police officer, pending successful completion of the police academy and a background investigation. I felt such elation it seemed as though I had just taken a fast trip to the moon and back at warp speed.

A friend of my parents who was in the mental health business told me years earlier, that I was too sensitive to work in law enforcement when discussing my professional aspirations with him. I would have none of his advice. There was a much bigger tug on my motivations than finding an occupation that fit into my sensitivities and personality. I wanted action and to be a hero, or at a minimum wear a blue uniform and carry a gun. It was the desire for adventure, the desire to conquer, to find an answer to the stirring of my soul, to satiate the thirst and the searching of my wild heart. God may have designed me to be sensitive but he also designed me with a desire for the adventure of life. My own perceived desires won the day in the end. It was truly one of the proudest experiences of my life leading up to the moment, when finally, after completing the academy, I put on my police uniform and proudly reported for my first day on the job.

A Sober Wake up to Deadly Reality

One of the most sobering days of my police career was one in which I wasn't even on duty. There was an experienced, older officer with whom I worked before he left our department and took a job in a much smaller one in an adjacent city. Jim had been offered a higher position in the hierarchy of the brass class. He also had become a friend. The quiet, quaint but posh little city on the shores of beautiful Lake Minnetonka in the Minneapolis metropolitan area, turned Jim's world into a violent and deadly one when one tragic day he unexpectedly found himself in a gun battle, out of nowhere, with some deranged maniac who had murder and mayhem on his mind.

Jim was brutally ambushed by the crazed individual. He was first shot in the hip, immobilizing him and rendering him nearly defenseless before being eventually assassinated in cold blood by the assailant. Another officer from my own department, as well as many other responders rushed to the scene where Jim had a moment of life left to call for back up help. Officers took up positions using the cover of their squad cars to confront the killer. My co-worker Ken was grazed with a glancing bullet to his fore head, thankfully inflicting only a minor wound. He was lucky that day. The gunman was eventually taken down but Jim was dead as was the assailant, making his cameo yet dramatic appearance in his insane world of darkness. There was a lesson to be taught in the grim reality of that day, that the danger and darkness of evil lurks anywhere it is allowed and it can strike without warning. Just because Jim had moved his police career to a seemingly quiet small town did not ensure his safety. Death can pounce and devour at any time in the least likely of places. It was a sad and sobering day. Most of my patrolman days were spent with much less traumatic, life impacting kinds of encounters, even having to endure many hours of restless boredom at times. There were some exciting times, interesting encounters, some hilarious moments, as well as unwanted boring stretches to contend with in my chosen line of work.

One of the stranger things that happened to me during my time on the Department, however, occurred one Christmas Eve morning when I was to work the day shift on patrol, not my favorite time to work. I much preferred working evenings and the night shifts just for the excitement value and action potential. Anyway, as my clock radio went off to the sound of some eerie new age music, I was having a very vivid dream where at a very specific place in my area of responsibility while on patrol that day, I saw a vehicle crash where a man was killed on the Interstate. I shrugged it off while experiencing a momentary reflexive chill but nevertheless went through my morning routine to then drive off to work in the pre-dawn dark.

At 7: AM our team hit the streets. About three hours later I received a radio call to respond to a possible fatal accident. As I approached the scene, I remembered thinking that this one looked awfully familiar as I observed a car jammed up against a concrete overpass buttress. Paramedics were already on the scene tending to what turned out to be a fatality though they told me the death of the male driver was caused by a heart attack and not the crash. But how did they know? These paramedics weren't trained to do autopsies on the street. His death was not trauma induced, they said, but he was dead just the same. At any rate, the episode got me to thinking because of the bizarre circumstances surrounding the event and my dream preceding it in the pre-dawn morning. There was clearly a mysterious element to the experience and it was a little disconcerting but it also contained an element of intrigue. I would have to file the experience away for a later time.

Grandma and Grand Tales

This kind of clairvoyant experience wasn't totally foreign to my world of understanding things, however. My maternal grandmother was a legitimate seer of future things. She told me of her experience in predicting her younger sister's death when they were kids. She also had the reputation of being able to predict where any fire was causing destruction in Milwaukee, where she lived later in her married life. She also never needed a clock in order to know exactly what time of day it was. She could see the time down to the minute.

When we were young, I remember taking trips to Milwaukee where my parents' families lived. I especially enjoyed going to visit with my Grandmother and Grandfather, but especially her because of the aura of mystery that seemed to surround her and to get her take on unseen mysteries of life. It was fun to listen to her tell her stories, always dressed in deeper and interesting colors of things unseen. One day she told me the sad tale of her younger sister when they were both young girls growing up in De Pere, Wisconsin, when the family was in the planning stages of a long-anticipated vacation. My Grandmother began having disturbed feelings one day and she sensed that for some reason they would not be able to go on their anticipated trip. Something ominous and dark was invading her thoughts. As time for the vacation drew nearer, her sense of some menacing yet unclear event grew clearer and stronger in her mind's sight. As the time drew very near to their anticipated departure, she told her parents something was going to happen that would preclude their going.

One morning she gazed at her sister, still asleep in bed, and said to herself, "it's you," sensing some foreboding event was going to involve her. That very day while her young sister was out playing, she impulsively ran into the street and was struck by a trolley car and was killed. Although the story ended in tragedy, my grandmother's telling of it filled me with intrigue and amazement. It was a convincing testimony to my grandmother's special gift and added to the mystery of life instilled in my young malleable mind.

She also told me one day when I was still in that very youthful stage of life that I would marry any girl which my heart desired, which struck me as an odd thing to tell a young person not yet anywhere near dating age. Her prophetic declaration to me sounded strange at the time and caught me by surprise. Her words, not forgotten, resonated stranger yet when I entered the Catholic seminary for my short career there years later in young adulthood. Roman Catholic priests are celibate. But at the same time, while progressing through the process of maturation, her prophetic message remained in the cognitive reflection of who I was. Her message empowered me and boosted my self-confidence around girls, even during that clumsy period of development when boys naturally feel awkward around girls. Her futuristic looking message, peering into my life not yet lived, felt to be almost a bad joke when years later I found myself trapped in a marriage that was clearly a mistake to be stuck in. One that was not life giving but life draining. But this story has not yet played itself out, so bear with me just a bit as we venture into the future, living the moments in successive order, giving rise to understanding and making sense of things. Moments of the present lived, which are the only ones to realistically savor and relish, because they are the only ones that we truly own.

Back to the Present

Let us rewind our focus to where we were before I got sidetracked, back to the dream and the fatal accident on the freeway I was trying to make sense of.

Years after that accident, foreseen in the early morning dream and later lived in real time for the second time, the phenomenon was explained to me. I was lucky to have a psychoanalyst to consult when Dr. Noreen Cannon was teaching a class I was taking while working on a graduate degree at Loyola Marymount University in Los Angeles. When I described my experience to her, she explained to me that our experience or knowing doesn't have to be in linear time (?). It can navigate outside that dimension. She was employing some quantum thought within Jungian psychology in which she had a P.H.D., but it was well outside my immediate wall of understanding at the time. I was not quite capable of knowing what she actually meant immediately, but I took her word for it and thought I'd have to ruminate on that a bit more for it to sink in. Finally, it has, to some extent. Funny how some things take years of chewing on before getting digested.

6

Running Again . . . To Escape

I resumed my running career during my early years on the police department. I think in part because I was restless, I needed a new goal, and it served as an escape from the mire I felt stuck in with the marriage I felt trapped in. At the time I could not seriously consider divorce. There were no serious issues whereby I could justify that to myself, besides, being raised in a traditional Catholic home, divorce was somewhat of a taboo. I just had to deal with my circumstances and a return to running offered a way to cope. . . and escape. This actually did justice to no one but it did offer itself as a temporary elixir in the moment.

    It became a salve and a crutch for me and I dove into it with renewed passion. I could lose myself in miles and more miles of gradual transformation into an intoxicating state with each mile logged. Addictive endorphins copiously released by my brain, lured my consciousness into a dream state where I could escape my reality. I would later wake up to the realization that living life truthfully is not running from it. But for the moment, it offered me space and a healthy direction of activity until I could get life's purpose and direction figured out. It was my temporary escape from the unresolved, tangled quagmire that needed sorting out. Run, run, run, think and reflect. I would get things sorted out and get what needed to get done, comforting myself with the imaginary thought.

    The more I ran the more attractive the idea of competing in the Twin Cities Marathon the following year became. The lofty ambition became more attractive in my thoughts which gave me a new beautiful mountain to climb and I dreamed of new vistas to view from on high. I set out on a very ambitious training regimen and by summer's end leading up to the marathon in the fall, I found myself to be in possibly the best running shape of my life. I was training in the company of elite runners and it was a great diversion from what I didn't want to face in my present domestic domain. It was a rewarding experience to realize new heights of progress and improvement in my now more mature yet still young body in its prime.

As time for the marathon drew very near, I felt an unwelcome change in my body that was disturbing. I started to feel sluggish and recall one day, while on a group ten-mile training run, that I was not only feeling as though I had led in my legs, but I was sweating profusely, more than what is normal. Fear that something significant was going haywire, I made an attempt to convince myself that maybe I had just been over doing it and I backed off hard training leading up to the race, hoping that all I needed was a little recuperation space. I was in denial but told myself a little recuperation time is a normal and smart tactic leading up to a major race anyway.

When the day arrived, I rose before sunrise and was at the starting line in downtown Minneapolis by 6:00 am. I started near the front of the pack. Self-placement among the crowd of competitors is a self-imposed proper protocol based on self-understanding of what level of runner one is. I knew I was perfectly capable of running close to five-minute miles based on the training runs I had logged, and had run, with the elite runners in my training group. I had reached my peak, but the nagging thought in the back of my mind that something was wrong physically remained with me. I pushed the thought away. But I was about to meet the cruel reality of defeat and humility head on. Because of my moderate doubt about my mysterious condition, I modestly lined up in the middle of the front group. Then we were off on the 26.2-mile sprint.

By the end of the first mile, I knew there was something terribly wrong. I felt as though I was running under water. I could not move the way I felt during my faster training runs which felt more like flying high in the air than running. As I plodded along, I struggled with my unwanted, horrifying thoughts as to what I should do. I had never quit a race in my entire racing career, even when not feeling optimal. At the risk of sounding sexist, at about the 13-mile mark the first female runner passed me and it demoralized me like nothing ever had in my life up to that heart crushing moment. I wanted to find an open man-hole in the street to crawl into and hide. Not finding a place to disappear into I just quit in a moment of mental anguish, frustration and confusion. I wanted to cry, to hide, to just disappear but could not escape from the confusing reality. Another blow and low moment in my experience of life, but once again, one to take a lesson from.

I actually cried tears of frustration, and loss (of something) later that day. They were tears of profound disappointment for all the effort I had put into preparation and the heights I had reached while training for the race. It was a heart wrenching moment and demanded a mountain of humility to face that reality of failure. I had a lot of friends out there expecting great things from me in the race. I let them down. I had lost my pride and was tortuously humiliated. How should one deal with such horrifying moments such as this one, I asked?

Re-entering Reality

It was about a month later that I noticed my body ballooning and it occurred to me that whatever the medication I had been taking for infertility issues at the time was really messing up my chemistry so I quit it abruptly. The steroidal medication probably was the cause for my physical misfiring and abrupt decline overnight leading up to and during the great race of my life, so I reasoned. Off the medication I began to lose the steroid induced weight gain and over the ensuing couple months began feeling normal once again. But in the meantime, I unfortunately allowed myself to get caught again by the dragon and was dragged back into its den of smoking cigarettes which piled onto the heap of feeling the sting of defeat. It only took one, in the desperation of the scent of depression, and I was caught again. The tradeoff for feeling normal again was consoling however, and I accepted the setback in the quiet still waters of temporary serenity by telling myself I could quit again.

So much for my escape into the dream. I suppose I could have rebounded and returned to that healthier dream of a serious athletic aspiration, but I concluded that life was calling me to face reality as it was being presented and to continue to journey on the mission yet to be clearly defined. Escaping into a dream was not what life's reality called for if seeking the truth is the goal aspired to. I continued to pray in earnest for an answer to my marital incongruencies. I was not being honest with myself about my direction in life and eventually would need to consult, in a very serious way, my personal compass. There I was . . . stuck, or should I consider the possibility of a new direction? I would need time to reflect on these matters. I needed to keep my sanity and live life honestly. What to do? What was the answer? At some point in my prayer, I felt as though I was getting a message that there would be a resolution to this quagmire, but I would need patience.

The more I prayed it seemed as though a message was coming into clearer focus and the number 40 years old began to emerge in my consciousness.

This fleeting thought was emerging out of nowhere and although I didn't know what I was supposed to think about it, that sudden notion or image that was coming forward was consoling in a strange way. It was like getting a reassuring message from God that things would get worked out, but not until you are 40 years old, so be patient. Not that I was necessarily getting a direct message from God but I do believe that he was working with my sub conscience in some way. I suddenly felt at peace with the gift of the present life and its contradictions even though forty was still a long way off.

It's entirely possible, on the other hand, that deep down I knew what I needed to do but was fearful of giving up the comforts of the status quo. I knew that separation causes suffering and it is human nature to avoid it at all costs. Besides, my kids were still pretty young and to shake up their world at this tender stage in life was not an appealing thought. Maybe my premonition had more to do with a hunch that with the passing of a few more years my situation would reach the level of crises that would eventually demand radical change and letting go. I decided for the time being to try to be content with matters in spite of living under the oppressiveness of control and reverse magnetic pulls away from natural inclinations for freedom and true direction of purpose.

7

Moving Forward into Mission and Imagination

My identity was still wrapped up in being a cop and the intrigue it had to offer, but within a few short years on the police department I started feeling restless. I needed to get creative to counter the feeling of stagnation I was suddenly beginning to encounter and struggle with. An innovative idea began to percolate in my mind about how to get involved in more creative police work. My idea evolved around the concept of establishing a proactive approach toward the investigation of narcotics and/or other "special investigations." The city had recently brought in a new Police Chief who had a reputation for being innovative and it didn't take me long to present to him my idea of creating a task force to conduct narcotics investigations and other special investigations of a pro-active nature; as opposed to just reacting to crimes that have already been committed, such as burglaries, assaults, or myriad other crimes that people commit. Up until then any narcotics or other proactive investigation was handled by the county narcotics unit or state criminal investigators from the Bureau of Criminal Apprehension (BCA). To my absolute delight the Chief accepted my proposal and sent me off to various relevant training courses.

A very significant and opportune course was being put on by the Drug Enforcement Administration (DEA). Also attending the class was a person who I immediately bonded with and who quickly became a new friend. Rick was a State Narcotics Investigator with the BCA. We hit it off during the class and it would ultimately prove to be an extremely fruitful relationship, significantly influencing events to be played out in the future. As well as in the rewards and joy of making a solid friend who had values and integrity. At the same time a new dream was being formed in my constantly dreaming mind. My thirst for new challenges was growing in my recurring desert of dryness again.

My newly found friend was a blessing on many fronts. Not only were we very compatible on different levels but he was generously anxious to get me established in the business of narcotics investigations. Having been a former State Trooper, Rick had developed the inclination and habit of driving like a mad man, yet while knowing how and having the skill to keep himself and those around him safe, he even put me on edge as he raced back and forth on the freeway that connected his office in St. Paul to mine on the west side of Minneapolis. I had taken advanced driving classes which teach very aggressive driving techniques to police officers that need those skills in carrying out their patrol functions. Rick used those techniques for just routine missions going from point A to point B, which made me uncomfortable as I suppose it also did for many of the vast number of commuters on the Twin Cities freeways. But that was his triple type-A personality, and for the sake of friendship, I just went along for the ride when riding with him.

Rick graciously offered, for my benefit, one of his informants who introduced me to a dealer of cocaine with whom I launched my narcotics police undercover career. The Minnesota Bureau of Criminal Apprehension, Narcotics Division provided me with enough money to buy a small amount of cocaine from the target. During the initial buy, surveillance agents connected my target to a "source of supply" who was a known narcotics trafficker in the sights of the DEA, as good fortune would have it. The next thing I knew the DEA entered into my virgin voyage into narcotics investigations and the seeds of a new adventure were planted. I couldn't have been more fortunate the way circumstances serendipitously played out and landed on my path, like charting along on the "Yellow Brick Road," I was singing the tune and clicking my heels in the air, like the trio of unlikely characters, and Dorothy in the *Wizard of Oz*.

We made a few more fairly substantial purchases of cocaine from my target, which were now funded by the Feds, in order to try to climb up the chain of supply and identify additional co-conspirators and sources of supply. Sadly, my target, as it turned out, was a Minneapolis school teacher who had fallen into the snares and unwanted or sought-after consequences of addiction. The DEA had been able to move up the chain of supply, identifying his source of supply and potentially the next level above him, so we took the case down, concluding my part in a successful "federal investigation." These cases rarely just end at this stage, but my undercover role in the matter was finished. It was all extremely providential from my perspective because I had established positive contacts with the Special Agents in the Minneapolis Resident office of the DEA, an office within the larger Chicago Field Division. This was big, real big!

DEA in my Sights, Locked and Loaded

A new dream had come to life in my world and the goal was to pursue the heights of becoming a Federal Agent with the Drug Enforcement Administration. After a long federal hiring draught, the DEA was finally accepting applications and I jumped on this potential opportunity with childlike enthusiasm. I had my supporters in the group of agents whom I had come to know through working with them on the cocaine dealer, school teacher case which had evolved into a respectable federal investigation with the Minneapolis Resident Office. The one female Special Agent in the DEA office was also the recruiter and she seemed to like me and supported my ambition and dream. This was a fresh, exciting time that also served well as a diversion from my marital relational issues. My wife actually supported me in my pursuit of this new quest, to my surprise. I was bubbling over with optimism and excitement.

After going through the hiring process that seemed like interminable waiting, I was, one day, notified that I had been accepted and, contingent upon successfully meeting the challenge and rigors of the DEA Academy, I would become a Special Agent of the Drug Enforcement Administration. I was warned that the academy was very challenging and that many candidates failed to make it through successfully. My class was somewhat of an experiment in that they leaned heavily on the recruitment of cops and former military, all who had successfully experienced the rigors of similar training and trials before. The hope with this strategy was to retain a larger percentage of their recruits as graduates than the usual.

Off to Quantico, Virginia I went in January to start a 15-week training experience that I would probably now term a training and "molding experience." I felt pangs of loss leaving my young adopted son and daughter for that length of time but I was determined to excel at this new challenge and opportunity. I was confident to the point of believing that I could graduate with number one honors, and in doing so be able to choose the office where I would initially be assigned. That would be back to Minneapolis to keep things domestically on an even keel.

Although I had not experienced basic training in the military, I think the "Academy" styled its psychological conditioning on the military model.

They try to beat you down before lifting you up, not allowing any sense of pride to seep in prematurely. By the end of the ordeal, however, that is the exact emotion I felt about successfully completing the process and almost graduating first in my class. But for a jammed toe that kept me from being successful enough in the 20-yard sprint shuttle during the physical test, I would have succeeded in attaining my goal. The disappointment in not being first in my class was only that I would not get my first choice for an initial field office assignment and therefore I would not be going back to my home office in Minneapolis. It did not dim my sense of accomplishment, however. In the long run it would prove to be a true unseen blessing. Life had yet many adventures to offer that I could not have even dreamed of at that time.

It had been a particularly harsh winter in Northern Virginia by their standards, very cold and unusually high amounts of snow fall, but coming from Minnesota I thought it was still rather balmy for a typical winter by my standards. By the time April and graduation arrived, the weather had turned warm and the sunshine was bright and comforting. The next few weeks were a whirlwind of activity, selling our house and finding another one in the Seattle area which would be my new home and workplace for the next five years. Seattle was second on my wish list based on a recommendation from my brother Mike, who had been a trucker early in his career and was familiar with just about every major city in the US. Everything seemed to go quite smoothly though, and by July we had moved to Seattle which I found to be incredibly beautiful with giant evergreen trees dominating the landscape of hills, water and snowcapped mountains. Giant Mount Rainier, covered in snow year-round, loomed to the south of us and could be clearly seen from the master bedroom of our new home. Best of all, the Western Washington winters were very moderate and much less biting compared to the extreme cold during those same months in the place of my birth. Seattle winters are rainy with occasional snow fall which might stick on the ground, at best, for a day or two, but they were to me profoundly temperate in comparison.

Having worked with the DEA in Minneapolis while still a local police officer, I felt quite confident in my ability to navigate my way through any challenges my new career might present and set out to prove that theory, and belief. My mission was my driving motivation and compelling purpose as I entered the newest phase on the journey of life.

8

Charging Forward, to Make a Mark

When I began work in my new career, in my new home office at the Seattle Division Office I was assigned to partner with Gary A, an agent with some experience and savvy. An Italian guy born in New York, with the requisite NYC accent, although later became mostly a product of Palm Beach, Florida. Gary was soft spoken yet smooth in demeanor like an underworld mob boss. We hit it off quickly and became friends, although I always felt that he was carrying some kind of extra weight on his shoulders that he didn't quite deserve. Maybe just the weight of life. I never figured that out about him. He was likeable in spite of his seemingly heavy heart though.

At the time Gary was working on a huge marijuana maritime smuggling case involving commercial cargo ships that were suspected to be US bound from South East Asia, allegedly smuggling the drug to Seattle and the West Coast. Much of my time was spent working in support of his investigation which from my perspective was a little boring but it was my first assignment and I relished the opportunity to be engaged in something so substantial although my instincts told me we didn't have much realistic chance of actually interdicting a contraband laden ship. The dream of it, however, fuels the motivation.

Armed with an abundance of enthusiasm for my new career I wanted more action and did manage to get involved in an undercover crack cocaine investigation before long, until eventually bigger and more exciting opportunities presented themselves. One perk working with my initial partner on his marijuana smuggling case though, was being able to fly up to and all around beautiful South East Alaska in a DEA piloted plane in search of a ship stuffed with marijuana, anticipated to be on its way to the U.S. from Thailand. The sights of our excursions included the powerful looking Mount McKinley and staring down from the plane to view glistening, brilliant, blue glaciers. This was God's country! Trying to spot a suspicious ship though, was like looking for a needle in a hay-stack, but the scenery was breath taking and the experience more than worth it.

From Calm to Calamitous

Before too long I was assigned to a new partner in a new enforcement group when the groups were re-shuffled. My new Spanish speaking Puerto Rican partner was a lively character and it wasn't long before we were involved in an investigation involving a Peruvian cocaine smuggling organization which was allegedly smuggling hundreds of kilograms of cocaine into the US from South America by way of the sea. It wound up being a wild and unnerving adventure that also presented me with the worst case of dysentery I had ever experienced in my entire life.

My Partner and I flew to Lima, Peru to meet with the Cooperating Individual (CI) who was a former Peruvian military officer. He somehow had the trust and confidence of the drug trafficking group, probably aided by the political environment at the time. The "Peruvian Mafia" was fighting against the communist insurgency, Sendero Luminoso, which was vying for dominance in the drug trade and the Government. The Peruvian Government and its military were for a long time in a conflict with Sendero Luminoso because it was attempting to destabilize the government and spread communist influence. The pseudo conservative leaning Mafia wanted to help the government in the struggle and therefore gain dominance in the drug trade. Each party had their own interest to promote but by diminishing Sendero's major source of income, drugs, both the legitimate government and the Peruvian Mafia would win. Sendero Luminoso aside, our target turned out to be the Mafia because of the strange dynamics and inroad he ironically had made with them. Complicated and strange sounding, but these are the type of alliances and weird dynamics conceived in the volatile marriage of drugs and third world national politics. The Peruvian Government, maintaining its smiley face in its own war on drugs, apparently chose to side with the U.S. in its war on drugs over the Mafia and its assistance in battling the communist insurgency. Thus, we had the paradoxical situation of a government official cooperating with us in an investigation, while simultaneously targeting both unholy ally and deadly foe. Maybe it was the case that the CI had a desire to ingratiate himself with the U.S. for a possible future life in the U.S. Whatever his motivation, human and political interactions are tricky at times, but we went with the momentum that was available to us.

We debriefed our retired military officer, CI, before being introduced to two of the Peruvian mafia-traffickers by him, posing as American buyers and distributors of cocaine. We had also met with a Group Supervisor from the Lima, Peru DEA Country Office to discuss and get approval for our game plan. We ended up falling on the wrong side of his supervisory prudential perspective in the end because we didn't communicate with him to his satisfaction. But we were working undercover in a Third World foreign country and wanted to keep our heads down to save our necks! What did he expect from two cautiously paranoid undercover agents working outside their environment in a tipsy-turvy country? Don't talk on the phone to anyone official was our advice to each other. The hotel phone (before the explosion of cell phones today) would be exclusively used to talk to the bad guys. It was good counsel we shared with each other, I thought.

The introduction to the traffickers involved having dinner with them at the rather swanky hotel where we were staying. The initial meeting was a get to know each other occasion in order to build up their comfort level and trust in that we were who we were purported to be. The meeting went well and they seemed to have confidence in us. The introductory dinner was followed up with several phone calls involving discussions about logistics surrounding a potential cocaine transaction while getting more familiar with each other. My partner was a master in his pretense and a slick talker. If he weren't an undercover DEA Agent, he could have certainly found himself a solid career in car sales or a shyster of some sort. Before we departed the following night, we agreed to meet again in the near future. The initial encounter seemed to go well, as far as making the pitch as to how we wanted to be perceived by them, fellow drug traffickers that were real.

I was feeling some uneasiness that these unknown drug traffickers knew where we were spending the night coupled with the fact that my partner was consuming far too much scotch whiskey. I was reliant on him for communication in this Spanish speaking country and was nervous about him losing his capacity for sound judgement and capabilities. Our second day in the country, my partner continued his binge drinking and I was starting to feel somewhat more panicked by the precarious situation. But he seemed to communicate well enough on the phone with our contacts from the night before and it seemed we parted company with them thinking we were the real deal and on pretty sturdy ground, coming across as legitimate traffickers ourselves, as best I could tell, not understanding what they were saying.

Over-all our initial contact with the mafia traffickers seemed to be a success, but with a price. We went to the airport that night for a very early morning flight back to Miami the next day. My partner crashed on the floor of the international terminal lounge area and I had some doubt as to my ability to rouse him on time in the few short early morning hours remaining before catching our flight. It was a bit of a nerve-wracking few hours but we made it onto the plane on time and I immediately felt a huge, wonderful sigh of relief once safely seated on that beautiful vehicle of assurance that we would get the hell out of there safely. Daniel (real name protected) slept deeply while I had other concerns. As things proceeded to go, as I did nonstop, there was little reason for me to have a reserved seat in the cabin section of the plane because I spent nearly the whole time on the lengthy three leg flight back to Seattle in the commode, painfully incapacitated. It was a trying trip and it felt wonderful to finally arrive back home late that night. It took a trip to the doctor the next day to get back to functioning properly again. Food poisoning in Peru!

Round Two with our Peruvian Mafia Friends

We had a follow up meeting with the traffickers in Guayaquil, Ecuador the following month without much of the drama we had previously, although, while having lunch in a restaurant on the second floor of the hotel establishment we suddenly heard gun shots ring out in the court yard below. From our vantage point there was no evidence of any victim(s) below, but it occurred to me that we were in the "Wild West" in this Third World South American city.

We had a third meeting with the "mafia" traffickers in Seattle several weeks later and were now getting down to the details of how this smuggling operation would unfold. Before our case came to its climax, however, we were informed that 500 kilograms of cocaine had been interdicted in Houston, Texas that was directly linked to our mafia friends and they were thus rightly busted. It might have been a Coast Guard interdiction at sea that interfered with our case. I never inquired about the details. But our undercover investigation was over. Justice was done. So much for dreams of DEA grandeur and fame early in my infant career.

9

Local Crooks Set the Course

The next adventure with DEA in Seattle was to go after a local trafficker who had stymied the federal and local narcotics law enforcement community for years. Back in the day when doing Title III, wiretap investigations was still a rare occurrence because of cost and man power considerations, I decided to pursue that route despite my boss's aversion to those kinds of investigations. Now days those investigations are much easier with improved technology and other advances, and are much more routine. I wasn't to be denied my quest, however. The idea had the support of upper management in the Division Office and my immediate boss was overridden, which did not make him a happy boss, but I was still brash and out to prove myself. I thought I knew better and probably did, but I didn't score points with him in that moment. He may not have been happy but neither did he resist. He was an adult.

Up we went on the "wire," intercepting the phone conversations of Ismael Barron, after the arduous process of writing a lengthy affidavit and making application for federal court approval. The wiretap was rather slow going at first but through conversations we went up on another line used by a rather large-scale heroin dealer out of Michoacán, Mexico, the Ariel Castaneda organization, relatively unknown in Seattle up to that time, which proved to be more productive. Ariel's line was hot and active and now we were juggling two entities, connected but on slightly different tracks, heroin from Mexico and cocaine on a more local scale. Barron's cocaine business wasn't producing much until we ran an informant, with the help of a Seattle Police Department co-worker, into the target to make several undercover purchases of cocaine. Now we were cooking because our defendant informant went to his supplier, Gorge Barragan. (The name is what my memory wants to tell me but it may not be precisely correct. It doesn't matter.)

He was a rather notorious trafficker known in Seattle narcotics enforcement circles, and the target of several different enforcement entities. He also had direct connections to Mexico, which is where he was from. Eventually we ordered up a substantial purchase amount of five kilograms of cocaine from him. Delivery of the drugs was prompt and smooth, a testament to the gravitas of our cooperating individual. Upon delivery of the drugs, we took the case down which resulted in numerous arrests and raids at numerous locations related to all the actors identified and involved. All in all, there were 55 kilograms of cocaine, approximately 11 pounds of Mexican black tar heroin seized, and 22 defendants arrested. A fast and furious climax to a long, slow-moving investigation, but that is how things go sometimes. A long and complicated trial in federal court was on the horizon.

After several months of preliminary court procedures and fastidious trial preparation, the six-week long event began. The lead federal prosecutor in the trial was small in stature, but fiery in personality and in his intense presentation of the case he made to the jury. He was a court room pit bull backed by the more cerebral assistant US Attorney who delivered an inspired summation in his closing argument at the end of the relatively drawn-out trial. At the conclusion, fifteen people were convicted. One, the wife of the Mexican heroin source of supply, Leticia Castaneda, was acquitted. Secretly, I felt happy for her, probably an innocent rural girl from Michoacán, Mexico, unwittingly dragged into the muddy mess by her trafficker husband, Ariel.

At least that is how her defense lawyers painted the picture for the jury. But it worked for me, so I was not surprised that the jury bought into the argument.

I was a little astonished at the heavy sentences that were handed down, but when you go to trial for six weeks and display a mockingly abundance of arrogance in federal court, the Judge may tend to get a bit more serious when it comes time to handing down sentences. There were pretty stringent sentencing guidelines she was obliged to follow, however. I felt pity for our original target, Ismael Barron and all those sent away that day as I sat in the courtroom and searched their faces. Barron looked old, tired and worn. In his late 60's already, he received a 60-year sentence and would never taste freedom again. This aspect of my job I did not relish or take any joy in. These misdirected lives were ruined but in the end what they chose to do was of their own doing and of their own free will. It was theirs' to deal with the consequences. The victims of drug trafficking and their preyed upon addictions by greed driven predators are adversely affected also, so I reasoned.

Flash to the Past

Reflecting on that moment in the Federal court room in Seattle, WA., did however bring to consciousness an experience I had on my St. Stephens grade school playground when I was in the fourth or fifth grade. It was always a fairly wild setting where anything goes as long as physical energy is spent so that the nuns could enjoy more docile and compliant students after hyper-active spent agents of learning and development might become more pliable and teachable afterwards. One day I went out to fulfill that requirement in my own unique way. Upon encountering a victim to accomplish what the nuns hoped for, to mitigate my own over active aggressions, I impulsively, with no thought, took this kid to the ground with an intuitive knowing the aggressive action had some higher purpose and meaning in life. It did. Even though he was older than me, thereby reasoning he was fair game, laying on his back in total surrender to me, his gaze into the eyes of my soul struck to the core of my being and in a flash jarred me into a state of reality that I was not accustomed to. In that moment of total transformative enlightenment, I felt a shock. It rocked me. I helped him up off the ground and with all the sincerity I could conjure up in that very youthful stage of understanding told him I was sorry, that he was really a good person and did not deserve to be bullied, especially by me. I thought about who else might come along and take advantage of his propensity for victimhood and weakness. Compassion for victims of the world broke through and blossomed in my heart that day in a dramatic experience of seeing pain in others. Our broken world has an overabundance of it. It would also shape the way I would deal with the encounters of the criminal slice of the pie I would meet in the future. There sometimes had to be force involved in trying to do justice, but that needed to include compassion. Lesson learned in the school of the raucous, raw, and rough training field of St. Stephen's playground.

Bobby Jones and Broken Bones

One of my favorite attorneys in the Seattle U.S. Attorney's office was Bobby Jones. I was drawn to his up-beat attitude, big smile and friendly demeanor. Bobby was always open to having a friendly conversation, about anything, in his office which was decorated with pictures and posters depicting a musical theme, in particular, jazz. One day we were shooting the breeze and talking about an upcoming ski trip my family was planning to embark on to Whistler Mountain, near Vancouver, Canada. I mentioned that I had never been there and wasn't quite sure how to get there. Bobby said, "hold on a minute.

I'll call my brother. He goes there all the time." Bobby dialed his brother up on his office phone and explained to him that I needed directions to Whistler Mountain. He then handed the phone to me. Bobby's brother was friendly and spoke with a rich, deep, smooth sounding voice as he gave me directions to Whistler. When finished, I thanked him and we hung up. After I did so I asked Bobby what his brother's name was and he replied, "Quincy." As in "Quincy Jones, the famous icon of the music world?" I asked. I had just had a casual, friendly conversation with the music giant, Quincy Jones. Bobby, in his typically smiling, boyish manner replied, "yeah." I said, "Oh man," slightly stunned.

We took off on our dream ski trip in mid-February when the day finally arrived, my mom having come from Florida to join us. My dad had just passed away the year before. I was feeling a little special on the drive to Canada, Whistler our destination, because of who the famous man who provided me directions was. It was a great time and beautiful conditions for skiing, with breathtaking scenery, until on the final day, cruising down the mountain, I stopped after hitting an icy patch to collect myself on the steep downhill slope. Standing sideways to the hill for a moment, I saw out of the corner of my eye, a split second before the crash, a huge guy who seemed to have a bull's eye on me. I took the hit to the outer portion of my left knee and went down, hard. I felt a sense of shock from the impact but didn't really feel too much more. Maybe that's like getting shot and not knowing it in the moment because of the shock effect. Getting myself back up, I observed I could not put any weight on my left leg, but dishonestly responded that I was okay when the couple asked if I was alright. Maybe denial or just trying to appear cool and not angry at the out-of-control big guy on skis. Maybe it was a little of both. He and his female partner continued down the mountain as I found myself making my way slowly to the bottom on one ski, then back to the top on a chair lift.

In the medical facility at the resort, I was informed that I had torn up everything, in terms of ligaments. All of them, anterior cruciate, bilateral ones and every other kind of ligament there is in one's knee to be destroyed; were. I was saddened by this news, because my very active nature was coming to a screeching, unwanted halt and my lifestyle was about to change in a significant way. This was a lifechanging event, or so I thought in that moment. It was a devastating experience, not so much because of the damaged knee, but because for the first time in my life my mortality suddenly became real to me. I recognized what vulnerability and frailty looked like as I drank a sobering dose of the ego shrinking cocktail. This new unfamiliar reality swept over me as the medical staff put a brace on my leg. I managed to drive back to Seattle thinking about how the new year would play out. I was a DEA agent. Could I still work?

I was fortunate to have possibly the best orthopedic surgeon in the region to repair my torn-up knee. He was the physician who was the orthopedic repair specialist for all the football players at the University of Washington and the Seattle Seahawks football teams. I trusted that he had an abundance of experience with those credentials. He did indeed work his magic and then I spent the next twelve months rehabbing, and to this day the knee feels great. Thank you, Dr. McCormick, amazing work and a blessing to have received your skillful care.

PART II

The Enchanted Land

Tectonic Life shifts on the Opposite Side of the Planet

10

Making a Move

Something new to brew presented itself unexpectedly. A fellow agent with whom I worked was back in Seattle on home leave after a year or so in his new assignment to the Rangoon Country Office in Burma, now known as Yangon, Myanmar. The DEA was planning to make an alteration to the very small office's make-up by adding one more Special Agent position and eliminating the current intelligence analyst position. My former co-worker in Seattle and friend Bruce, strongly encouraged me to put in for the opening. He set forth a rather enticing sales pitch pertaining to the country itself, as well as the working environment and living conditions. He emphasized how safe it was for families, how friendly the people were and the very interesting work with minimal danger involved. Living was good there, he enthusiastically exclaimed.

The work was mostly of an intelligence nature, so it involved a lot of writing and interviewing a network of informants who regularly provided intelligence on the vast and immense poppy production in that region known as the "Golden Triangle." In particular was Burma's hefty proportion of production of the drug in the region at the time. The Golden Triangle also included Thailand and Laos. From poppies opium is extracted and from opium heroin is produced. The country at the time was still very much un-unified due to the segregation of many distinct, separated ethnic groups with somewhere in the area of 135 distinct dialects spoken. The mountainous and rugged terrain contributed to the lingering segregation of the many ethnic groups as did also the strong cultural distinctions and diversity among them. Although there wasn't much internecine conflict among them anymore, there was fierce fighting between several of the ethnic groups and the Military Government of Burma. Many had made peace pacts with the central government but a few remaining outliers such as the Shan Chinese, who produced opium, and the Karen ethnic groups, who did not. The Karen, a people who had maintained the longest insurgency in Burma's history, now nearly 75 years and on-going, were divided by religious affiliation, Buddhist and Christian as well as by their own distinctly different languages, but yet remained the same ethnic people by blood line.

The insurrectional conflicts largely took place far away from the major cities in the more remote and rural areas of the country. It was the ultimate goal of the Central Government to eventually unify the whole country under the Military Junta's umbrella and bring the remaining fractious, rebellious ethnic groups into peace accords with the Government. There remained, however, substantial resistance and on-going skirmishes with the Burmese Army in several areas throughout the country. All of this conflict had very little bearing on our work however, and the city of Rangoon was a safe place to do our work and live, according to my friend. We just needed to avoid the conflict areas which the government pretty much assured anyway.

After my years in active and sometimes intense, enforcement work, this kind of assignment sounded very appealing and attractive to me at the moment. Besides, there were certain financial benefits to working in a foreign office, especially one considered a "hardship" post. First of all, there was subsidized housing and hardship incentives, mostly provided in Third World country assignments with few amenities that living in the US would normally provide.

Selling a Whopper

Now I had the no small challenge and task to go sell this potential adventure to my wife. I was lining up and rehearsing my selling points: The school situation was excellent where she could likely get a job teaching at the American International School, there were plenty of wholesome activities for the kids and they could make plenty of new friends among all the various diplomatic families from around the world providing cultural diversity. We also could save some extra money due to the low cost of living and subsidized housing. Furthermore, we could rent out our house in Redmond, Washington for additional income. This was a well plotted out delectable and sumptuous sales pitch, I thought, and I was pretty confident this was going to be a slam dunk! At least I had myself sold on the idea, thinking that was a reliable barometer.

After sufficiently rehearsing the proposal in my mind, the grand presentation was made. To my surprise and delight, it went pretty smooth. My wife initially seemed fairly agreeable, but first things first. I needed to get selected for the job. Apparently from the in-house DEA perspective Burma was not generally viewed as an attractive place to go because it was a far-away, remote Third World Country. And fortunately, because of that, competition for the assignment was minimal. From most points of view the assignment had little sex appeal. In fact, my only real competition for the job consisted of just one other agent within the Seattle Division office who was very interested in getting an assignment somewhere in South East Asia. He was senior to me which I thought might give him the advantage. My advocate and counter advantage to him, however, was Bruce, who was already well established in Burma and had done two previous foreign tours of duty in Bangkok, Thailand; and I was his choice to work with. He told me Burma was a well-kept secret and many people were just not aware of the Country Office and what it had to offer. I think he convinced the Rangoon Country Office Attaché, Angelo Saladino to pitch me to the Foreign Operations Division in DEA Headquarters. I was ultimately selected for the position at last and felt as though a grand chapter was about to open before me. My competition, Ed, was selected for an opening in the Hong Kong, China Country Office shortly thereafter which made me feel happy for him and his wife, who probably preferred the idea of going to Hong Kong over Burma anyway.

There were obstacles to overcome, however. My Korean adopted son was 10 years old at the time and had been diagnosed as having a mild case of Asperger's Syndrome, which causes people with the disability to perseverate on things making teaching them in school a bit more of a challenge. They also have some difficulty in social relationships. In other words, their focus gets stuck on things and they display symptoms of mild autism. In my son's case it wasn't severe so it wasn't a huge challenge for him but he would need a special medical clearance from the State Department because of his unique condition. That was a bit worrisome for me, but it must have been God's providential will for us to go to Burma because eventually, after scouring personnel manuals and presenting the right arguments to the right people, he was given a conditional State Department medical clearance and we were off to the enchanted land in South East Asia.

Adventure, Adversity and Adjustments

When my wife was in her twenties, she began displaying mental health issues that were somewhat disturbing and confusing at the time. She was smelling things that weren't there to smell and seeing things that weren't there to see. A neurologist had her check into the Psychiatric Ward at the University of Minnesota Hospital for an evaluation. She thought the psychiatrist evaluating her had evil designs intending to do her harm. It was perplexing and disturbing to hear her talk and act outside the boundaries of what I thought was "normal." After several days of evaluations and medications she was released. Her neurologist told us that his "official" diagnosis was that she was experiencing some sort of nominal brain seizure activity, to obfuscate and minimize her real condition so as not to handicap her with some potential stigmatizing, more severe diagnosis. The anomaly eventually passed and was largely forgotten, or more accurately suppressed. Her paranoiac symptoms abated but she would occasionally display bursts of unexplainable aggression that were unsettling. I remember a priest and former college friend of mine came to visit us in Seattle for a couple days. He was the Rector at the Collegium Josephina Seminary in Columbus, Ohio. A seminarian under his tutelage was being ordained a priest in Yakima, Washington and Blasé wanted to be there for his student's major life event. He stayed at our home and I drove him to Yakima for the ordination. While at our house my wife had one of her unexplained occasional explosive outbursts which seemed to come out of nowhere and for no rational reason. Blasé would comment on the incident years later after the divorce. It apparently left an impression on him at the time.

As time drew near to head over to Burma many years after those early warning signs it appeared that now something more serious was going on with her mental health. She again began displaying disturbing signs of paranoia. I was probably in a bit of denial myself because I did not want to face the reality of what might have actually been going on with her and I chalked up her paranoid thought patterns to just simple anxiety and stress over the looming life altering move. At least this is what I convinced myself was going on and I made numerous, patient attempts at reasoning with her that everything was going to be just fine, rationalizing to myself that once we arrived and got settled everything would be good. I was running the race of my life toward reaching the goal that was Burma, and was missing some of the alarming warning signs posted along the road which led there.

I didn't see what was coming, I fooled myself into justifying her paranoia by chalking it up to the stress of making such a huge change in our lifestyle and getting things prepared and organized for the move half way around the world. Heck, we made a major move from Minnesota to Seattle just a few years earlier and that proved to be a smooth one involving no psycho altering detours or impediments. Somehow though, I sensed ominous clouds forming, but was determined to make all things well, and charged ahead. Staying positive seemed the wisest posture to take. We had rented our house out, purchased a years' worth of consumables, because buying food on the local market wasn't advisable, and made all other arrangements for the transition. We were ready for the adventure . . . at least I was.

The Arrival, the Unfamiliar, and the Heat

We arrived in Rangoon, Burma, (now known as Yangon, Myanmar), in the afternoon, March 19, 1992, on the Feast of Saint Joseph and anniversary of my grandmother's death. I thought that was significant and auspicious in and of itself. At the time Burma was still very much a Third World Country, although it has developed exponentially since then. A popular mode of transportation around the city of Rangoon and the country was still by rickshaw, a three-wheel bicycle with a bench seat in the back for passengers. I quietly admired the skinny operators who powered the vehicles with their scrawny legs, even up hills, with apparent ease. Modern automobiles were rare in the city and the ancient dilapidated buses from the 1950's, and more modern ones from the 1960's, often listing to one side or the other, continued to breath gasps of life while plying the by-ways, overly stuffed with human beings on the inside, with many people hanging on to the side of the relics on the outside.

The country was just entering into its "hot season" when we arrived in March. It was, in fact, downright oppressive in relation to the Pacific North West of the United States which had become our climactic comfort zone in the temperate, cool air of Seattle. Two days after arriving on Friday, we walked the six blocks from our temporary place of residence on Sunday to the nearby Catholic church for Mass. We were cooked and soaked with sweat upon entering the church, which had no air conditioning. I wasn't making an immediate, favorable impression on any member of my family as to the pleasantness of life in Burma on that outing. The heat was a mild shock. There are three distinct seasons in Burma; the "hot season" which we were beginning to experience, the "rainy season," and the "cool season." Arriving at the church, frazzled, hot, and beaten down by the oppressive heat, our collective minds were far from being focused on what they should have been for the next hour.

Angelo, the Country Attaché, had welcomed us the day of our arrival, having shown up at our place with a television and DVD player for our use. The following evening, we made the short walk over to Angelo's, and wife Barbara's residence, minus the noon day sun beating down on us. Unfortunately, in the middle of the lovely steak dinner I was overcome with nausea and had to urgently jump up from the table and run outside to make a mess on the garden bushes. What a way to make a first impression! Angelo and his wife were gracious and understanding, pretending that nothing had happened. I surmised, upon reflection, having just made an abrupt, massive cultural, and dramatic time zone change, combined with the stress setting in over concern for my family's difficult adjustment, that it just may have been a normal bodily reaction to it all. Angelo told me the bushes would be fine.

Changes, Unwelcomed and Welcomed

Regrettably, Angelo was due to leave soon as his tour of duty was nearly over. He seemed to be an exceptionally nice guy to work for and although I didn't get a lot of time to spend with him, he left a lasting impression on me regardless. I think Angelo was under a lot of pressure from the folks at our Foreign Operations Division at DEA headquarters in Washing D.C., especially the chief of the Division who had a beef with the CIA and dragged Angelo into the middle of it. He just wanted to get along, so it seemed to me. Angelo struck me as somewhat beaten down and frayed at the edges. When he left for the States, he was replaced by Rick, who had a much less agreeable personality and seemed right off the bat to be a somewhat combative person. Rick had foreign experience working in Lahore, Pakistan, which is rough and not known as a nice place. In the end though, he did me no harm on either a professional or personal level but he certainly looked as though he had a disposition to do so if he were so inclined. I figured our relationship would not have to endure any substantial length of time because he appeared to be looking for a fight with both the CIA and State Department. I knew who would come out on top in that face off. It didn't take him long before he was quickly at odds with the CIA Station Chief and upper-level embassy brass. He had to know with his foreign experience that the Ambassador, or Charge d' Affaires has the final word on who is in or who is out. Rick pushed the envelope a little too hard and he found himself in the "out" category. I didn't have to endure too much stress worrying about his unpredictable, explosive tendencies because it did not take long at all before he was packing his bags. I knew it was coming but was a bit surprised that it took nearly one year before he was finally sent packing and tossed out of the country. Typical State Department, delicate touch at play, I suppose.

That left Bruce and me to run the office. He took over as Acting Country Attaché for a while but must have gotten on the wrong side of somebody at DEA Headquarters because to my huge surprise and chagrin, they designated me Acting Country Attaché. I found myself in the very awkward position of Bruce, my senior by a long stretch and with loads of foreign DEA experience, suddenly becoming my subordinate. It was very uncomfortable for both him and me. On a personal relational level this arrangement was awkward to say the least and cast a chill on our normally warm relationship.

Bruce retreated from any normal interaction, having become very aloof and non-engaged. It carried over into his professional demeanor as well. He just kind of went AWAL but his tour was about to come to an end anyway. Bruce departed Rangoon soon thereafter and I found myself in Burma by myself to represent the DEA. He and I had not talked about the strange confluence of circumstances that caused his falling out of favor with DEA Headquarters largely because he chose reclusiveness over communication. He probably felt hurt and betrayed, by whom, I'm not sure. Headquarters didn't shed any light on the situation for me either. Okay, I said to myself. Live where you are and with the circumstances you are left with. I was still happy to be in Burma.

Within a couple of months Gary Carter arrived as the new Country Attaché along with his welcomed and accompanying reputation for being a very likeable and easy-going person. When he did arrive, he was initially very reliant upon my accumulated knowledge of the Country; its politics, and our operation in Burma, which I had acquired over my two plus years there.

But here I have gotten way ahead of myself. I need to rewind the clock a couple of years back to the general time frame to where we were shortly after our arrival in Burma. There was at that time a much more significant drama playing out in my turbulent life, in the trauma dominated era of successive bad dream days. The stark, dark reality of complexity and confusion had been gradually mounting into an inescapable nightmare in the drama playing itself out, beginning with small waves of turbulence, building into catastrophic ones, crashing down in violent explosions, and threatening to sink the ship of my life and of those on it.

Storm Clouds Building

Shortly after our arrival in Burma, my wife's symptoms of paranoia began to manifest themselves in much more dramatic fashion and it started to alarm me in a serious way. She had been offered a job at the International School teaching music in the fall. I didn't have much doubt that she would because she was very talented at what she did and it was readily noticed by anyone who knew the business. I thought re-engaging in her profession might bring her back into the realm of reality, at least the way most of us perceive it. During the Spring and summer monsoon season, however, she became convinced that the CIA had concocted some sinister plot to gain control over our son Tim and that I, strangely, was somewhat complicit in the wildly imagined arrangement, or at a minimum had some capacity to do something to mitigate the nefarious scheme. It started to spin into realms of delusion that I could not even find empathy for, as hard as I tried to imagine where she was coming from. She was breaking badly and suddenly from reality and it scared me beyond telling, especially finding myself in the unfamiliar, far away land with new surroundings and people.

My wife, Kate, did start teaching music at the American International School in the fall but it was only a matter of weeks before things began spiraling out of control and were rapidly unraveling. She had been selected to attend an education conference in Pattaya, Thailand, which I thought would do her good and get her mentally reconnected and engaged. But within the first or second day of the conference, all hell broke loose. And from what I later observed, I mean Hell! The kind that is very scary and where nobody in their right mind wants to go or dares to think about going.

I received a shocking call from the American Embassy in Bangkok asking me to come and rescue her, or them, I'm not sure. I just knew it sounded like whatever the situation, it had taken on urgent and emergency level proportions. I struggled to imagine what in this bad dream was actually playing out, but it sent me into a state of panic that was hard to contain within disintegrating walls of stability, which I struggled to maintain. There were no consoling thoughts whatsoever, that I could conjure up in my imagination that could make this scenario less frightening. I was fighting mightily to just stay in the moment and do what needed to be done. Walk into Hell and try to find a way out, was my interpretation of the situation.

I was lucky to catch the second, late afternoon flight from Rangoon to Bangkok, which is about 40 minutes or so in the air. Upon arrival, I was met by a DEA Investigative Assistant (A Thai national, embassy employee) who drove me to Pattaya. I experienced debilitating levels of anxiety during the hour and a half drive not knowing what I was going to find. I just knew it could not be good.

When I walked into the building where she was residing, I was shocked at the sight, which looked like a war zone. Apparently, Kate had become extremely disruptive and violent, according to witnesses and the appearance of the destroyed room that she occupied. It looked like a Texas sized tornado had just torn through it. I had no idea what kind of horrific thoughts or fears, which had taken over control of her mind, could possibly be cause for such violent and unprovoked behavior. The place was a visible disaster that told a vivid horror story of what was going on inside her head. I was shocked into speechlessness when initially setting eyes upon the utter chaos of objects and clothing thrown about all over the place. I tried to engage her with some calm rational conversation but she was too far gone into an unreachable, disturbed, other world to even come close to connecting. I don't think she even recognized me. The crazed look on my wife's face shocked me into near incapacitation, but I moved forward. Her eyes were unfocused, glazed over and wild as she hurled swear words at a guy, who at the time I took to be a priest. I guess the staff had called him in to assist, at her apparent request, although I don't know why she had asked for a priest because when I arrived, she was cursing and throwing things at him as though he were the devil himself. Maybe the devil took up temporary residence in her and wanted to attack the ordained one. Those kinds of otherworldly battles, I'm not equipped to explain.

A medic and a doctor arrived in an ambulance and were able to get her calmed down by medicating her, although, in the midst of that chaotic scene everything was a blur and details elude me. I was a bit traumatized and scared not knowing who to turn to or what was to come next. But not much of anything surprised me anymore.

It was by now pretty late in the evening and during the dark, hour-long or so drive back to Bangkok, Kate fell into a medicated induced sleep while my head was spinning. I was just thankful that she was now quiet and no longer in a frightening state of rage. I was also extremely thankful for the DEA investigative assistant who drove me to Pattaya and both of us back to Bangkok. That is a testament of dedication and kindness on the part of the Embassy in Bangkok and my new Thai friend who's name I don't even know. Besides those names are too long to possibly remember anyway.

We stayed at a hotel in downtown Bangkok not far from the American Embassy that night. The following day Embassy staff sent a doctor over to the hotel to check on us, although he didn't shed too much light on the situation at the time. He simply brought reinforcements in the way of medication for her which basically caused her to sleep through the day and the following night. We went out for a walk the next day and happened to pass by the newly built, smart looking American Embassy compound. Kate was insistent on seeing the Ambassador. And now I had a problem to somehow deal with. I think she felt she needed to inform him of the evil plot being devised against her and my son up in that evil place, Rangoon.

She had a mind of her own, disoriented as it was, and it took all my persuasive effort to dissuade her from attempting to get to the Ambassador's residence inside the Embassy compound. But in the end, I prevailed, thanks in large part to the fortified security fence surrounding the complex. She had enough reasoning capability, apparently, to figure out that getting inside was not going to be an easy task given the physical security challenges. Or maybe it was just the heat and her own weariness that took over. Whatever the reason, I was just, at the moment, extremely thankful for security structures and their architects.

The thought was a dominant one in my mind that up to this point in my life I had never felt so totally out of control over a situation. It was an awkward one. Frightening, like being lost at sea with no compass, not knowing what to do or which way to steer my ship to safe ground, from the vast and turbulent ocean I was lost in. Panic was the dominant feeling and the distasteful flavor of life at the moment, but deep down I knew it would all work out. Just take the next step. I had been down this kind of treacherous, cratered highway before.

11

Return Trip Back Around the Planet

We returned to Rangoon the following day and a few days after that I had a talk with the Embassy physician, Doctor Broadbent, in his office. Paul was a very genial person who sincerely wanted the best for my wife and my family. He was easy to talk to and we had a constructive and calm inducing conversation. I dearly needed that at the time. Together we decided the best plan would be to return to the States and seek psychiatric consultation. I had been in country for six months and was eligible for a Rest and Recuperation (R & R) visit which spared me from having to pay out of pocket for rather expensive airline tickets back to the States. Instead of returning to Seattle we made plans to go to Minneapolis where we could stay with my brother and his wife and have the comforting support of family. I was grateful for that and it provided ample comfort and assurance in the void and the untethered insecurity in that far away Asian land. We left the kids in Rangoon to continue with school, in the trusted care of our domestic helpers.

There was already chill in the air as we arrived in Minnesota, in the latter part of October when things start to cool down for the always expected fast-approaching winter, but it felt warm and a huge relief being in the company of supportive family members. Kate had no more severe psychotic breaks for the time being but the paranoia lingered. The psychiatrist we consulted used the words paranoid and schizophrenic, which seemed to fit the equation in my mind. He treated her with psycho medication of some sort and after a few days she seemed stable enough to return to Burma. There were no more shock inducing incidents for months after our return, but she was clearly not right, as in being her normal, former self, but I gratefully accepted the fact it was a calmer more functional self. I just thanked God for the sweetness of calm.

Signs of Reality in Retrospect

An article appearing in the Hillsdale College Publication *Imprimis,* adapted from a speech delivered on January 15, 2019 by Allan P. Kirby Jr., Center for Constitutional Studies and Citizenship in Washington D.C., addresses the link between psychosis and violence. Berenson cites the website for the National Alliance on Mental Illness (NAMI) quoting their statement: "Most people with mental illness are not violent." Berenson goes on to say however, "but wishing away the link can't make it disappear. In truth, psychosis is a shockingly high-risk factor for violence." He bases his statement on a paper in *PLOS Medicine* by Dr. Seena Fazel, an Oxford University psychiatrist and epidemiologist. "Drawing on earlier studies, the paper found that people with schizophrenia are five times as likely to commit violent crimes as healthy people, and almost 20 times as likely to commit homicide."[1] This would have been useful information for me back then. But then again, I was at the time in a state of confusion and some denial, slow to readily accept that there was something other than a tendency for "normal" going on in Kate's mind and behavioral patterns. Confusion is understandable, denial also, because I wanted to experience normal.

The following school year she returned to teaching at the International School and our routine settled back into relative normalcy while we grew accustomed to life in Burma. After two years had passed, my tour was up. Things had been going well and were stable enough for the kids and Kate, that we put in for a second two-year tour. On our Home Leave between tours, we went to Clearwater, Florida where my mom lived, and still does. We stayed with her in her rather large house built for a large family of eight children, and for many years, the place accommodated many different combinations of family visits as well as friends and other visitors who may have needed a place to rest their heads.

Kate was beginning to display disturbing symptoms of paranoia and aggression again. One day for no apparent reason, she took my golf clubs out of the trunk of our rented car and flung them across the parking lot toward the doctor's office we had just seen for her now recurring symptoms.

My feelings about her paranoid and aggressive behavior began to turn from sympathy and empathy into ones of anger and impatience. The

1. Berenson, "Marijuana, Mental Illness, and Violence."

doctors she visited while on leave in Clearwater adjusted her medications which curbed her aggression but also had the negative side effect of turning her into a zombie like character. Personality was virtually ripped from her personhood. She was functioning adequately, but she appeared to be just sleep-walking, totally void of any animation. It was a sad sight to behold, superficially content, aggression suppressed, but life departed for some other place to where I could not see or understand. I totally did not know where she was and I'm not sure she did either. Welcome to the world where psychotic suppression and robotic existence meet.

The Truth Will Set You Free

A year into our second tour we were back in the States for another R & R and after stopping in Seattle and Minnesota we eventually made our way back to Florida. I took the liberty of a much-needed visit and consultation with my Uncle Jack, friend and life-long mentor who happened to also be a counselor. He and his wife lived in a spacious, airy condominium seven stories up, overlooking the beautiful Gulf of Mexico on Clearwater Beach just a few minutes' drive from my mom's house. I needed his wisdom and advice. I had no one else to confide in and felt quite alone when it came to sharing life's perplexing encounters on a deeper level. I drove to their condo complex by myself so that I would have the luxury and freedom to discuss matters of deep concern about the complex world of being human. I knew I was on the precipice of facing some kind of life correction and needed to bounce that befuddling reality off someone who I trusted, respected and who also knew me as a person.

    I talked to Jack about the alienation and pain I felt in my marriage, where any kind of meaningful relationship should be alive and realized, but instead was void and empty. Empty to the point of insult to her and me because it was not living life truthfully. Void of physical, interpersonal intimacy or meaningful interaction of any kind, negating any iota of joy which should be present to some degree in any real marital relationship. In my understanding, a sacramental union designed by the Creator of all things, is meant to reflect Trinitarian love, relational existence. That's my sincere theological and philosophical take on the matter. I'm not quite sure I necessarily articulated those feelings with that specific level of sophistication, but my sentiment and thoughts at the time were consistent with that idea. After a slightly clumsier presentation and words that dribbled out in his welcoming living room overlooking the ocean of calm water, I had rendered my feelings and concerns to him as best I could. His profound response was simply: "You better go find a mistress." That was not the wise response I would have expected from this often-profound thinking man but he did unleash in me a fresh way of perceiving and thinking about my situation over time.

While I did not immediately go out and put his words to practical application; from his seemingly glib response, a hidden message containing profound advice was revealed, and it did ignite a spark toward re-engineering my thought process away from the super ego of Should(s) and Should Nots, toward a deeper reflection on the notion of "authentic self," and a true northward look at the direction of my life. My navigation system was about to make a radical readjustment and the time for a sharp turn was just around the blind corner ahead.

We returned to Burma to begin the final leg of my final assignment there. During the final months, there were no harrowing, traumatic, psychotic events encountered, giving space and air to breath for the life changing decisions which needed to be made and the plans formed to be actualized. It was in fact boring on the drama front but significant on the sober decision making one. Kate had lost her personality entirely to her illness and requisite medications.

There was one singular hair raising and disquieting moment, however, when on a delightful evening with warm tropical air engaging my senses in soft, friendly visits of gentle breeze passing into the kitchen through the window in front of the sink where I was happily engaged in doing dishes after dinner. I suddenly felt as one experiences before a close encounter with a lightning strike. The hair on the back of my neck stood up in instantaneous and self-preservation reaction. In that milli-second, all my senses screamed: "Danger!" I turned around and found Kate standing behind me wielding a large butcher knife, staring at me with a menacing look on her face. I uttered something to confront her and she turned and walked out of the room. Right then and there, I said to myself, enough . . . this relationship is over. It really had been for quite some time however, but this moment had a feel of finality and surety to it. I had reached, in that moment, a point where I found the clarity of truth about our marital relationship which had suddenly come into hyper focus. The relationship that really wasn't, just could not be sustained in its superficial and tortuous state any longer and I needed to make that perfectly clear. In that moment of brute honesty with myself I also experienced a sense of fortitude and strength rising up within me. I felt a sense of liberation and peace wash over me, although I intuited there would be stormy waters ahead. But now in that moment of truth and resolution I was ready to face the turbulence. I felt free and a certain exhilaration setting in.

12

Recalling Beauty not Lost in Living

In spite of the trials and challenges that accompanied them, I still absolutely loved Burma and life there. I had the privilege of being allowed to travel to many parts of the country with the Burmese military, areas which were largely off limits to other foreigners and diplomats because of insurgencies and conflict. The DEA had a special kind of privileged relationship with the military, who at that time had a tight grip on the functionality of the country and government. There seemed to me to be a certain magical enchantment about the country in spite of that. The ancient pagodas and culture of the Burmese people provided a certain serenity that was unique and to which I was strongly attracted. Whenever I travelled back to the US, I inevitably could not wait to return to Burma. The people were very hospitable and there was a gentleness and politeness in their demeanor which was endearing. I was drawn to their culture and life which engaged me with its charm. The country is predominantly Buddhist which draws one into a spirit of gentleness and peacefulness. Not that there aren't the same human failings and faults that prevail throughout the whole human condition in the world, but Buddhism does have a calming effect on the outward cultural face of a society where it is predominantly practiced. It is appealing and attractive. This face of peace for me at that time was a salve that soothed the more contradictory aspects of my situation.

And then there was Golf

I had dabbled in playing golf throughout my lifetime but had never seriously worked at it. Playing golf in Burma was a serious endeavor and became an elixir and a wonderful diversion for me. Before we originally departed for Burma, my friend Bruce advised me to bring golf clubs because playing golf was a big deal there, in addition to the fact there was not a whole lot of other activity to engage in, except that which the American Club had to offer. That mainly amounted to tennis, swimming, softball, eating and drinking. No thanks. I opted for golf, although I did casually engage in softball, swimming, eating and drinking at the American Club. It was a great place for families and kids to hang out, have fun and get to know people.

Burma had been a colony under British rule from 1824 until finally obtaining their independence in 1948 after the Japanese occupation during the Second World War. The Brit's did not waste time establishing golf courses in many parts of the country, especially in the more populated areas. The golf courses varied in degree as to how manicured they were, from very rough to not bad at all. I dove head first into the sport, actually reaching a decent level of playing proficiency before leaving the country. It was so affordable it would have been remis to not take a poke at it if one was only even a bit inclined to do so. The characteristic thing about playing golf, and the challenge of it, is that you can never stop trying to improve in the never reachable goal of reaching perfection. Just as in being human, we strive for perfection but never quite get there, in this life anyway.

It was a wonderful past time, challenge and an attractive diversion which took my mind off other more life draining concerns. The golf course was a life-giving playground. I thought of it as a gift and took as much advantage of the opportunity as I could get away with. It was extremely affordable in Burma and was a great way to interact with the local people. The Burmese people whom I played with took the sport seriously and were good at it so I had to become proficient. It also provided pleasing aesthetic encounters outdoors in the lush tropics. I had a new passion in life. Or another diversion maybe? I wasn't too concerned about that though.

Playing with Burmese friends and professional counterparts was also a large part of the extracurricular package. My playing partners included members of the Burmese police and Military Intelligence (DDSI) with whom we worked. One particular day a jolting irony occurred on the occasion of playing at a small course on the outskirts of Rangoon. We were following a group of players in the group just ahead of us which I later discovered included a former infamous drug trafficker and former leader of the Kokang Chinese insurgent group, Lo Hsing Han, who had earned designated "Kingpin" status by the U.S. Government. Lo, within DEA circles was a well-known high-profile former trafficker of heroin and opium. I was very familiar with his profile while I was still working in Seattle. He and his band of insurgents had, some years earlier, made peace with the Government and was now welcomed into the main stream of Burmese society and were given a pass for past misdeeds.

So, there was the irony, a world-famous drug trafficker in my DEA world, playing golf in the group ahead of the group which included a DEA agent. This was a paradox to me, because back in Los Angeles, there were DEA agents still diligently working to make the case to get him indicted for his former infamous drug trafficking activity. It presented a funny contradiction to me, but those are the humorous ironies of life. Later in the club house, his group of playing partners was having a celebration because Lo, now an old man but proficient golfer, had just scored a hole in one on one of the par-3's. Lucky day on the Chinese calendar, I guess.

Visit from a Hero

As I am here today, just having watched on TV all the beautiful memorials and funeral of the renowned and perplexing Senator John McCain from Arizona, I reflect back on the time he and his CODEL came to Burma on a fact-finding mission. There was a cocktail reception for him and his entourage hosted by the Charge d' Affairs on a Saturday evening which the DEA Country Attaché, Rick and I attended. I met Senator McCain there and found him to be a somewhat friendly yet serious man.

The next morning, Rick and I were asked to conduct an informal briefing for him and have an in-depth discussion concerning DEA's ability and effectiveness in working with the Burmese Government on narcotics issues. I guess I was asked to attend because of my accumulated knowledge of the complex history of Burma's ethnic internecine conflicts and its influence on the country's booming and historical opium production. It was a quiet, yet lively discussion. John McCain's questions were serious and probative. My impression of him at the time was that he was a seriously inquisitive person sincerely attempting to gain an understanding of how to address the complexities of the US's engagement with Burma on the foreign policy front. At the time, the ruling Military Junta that ruled the country had some serious human rights issues in the perspective of the US and relations were not particularly rosy. The DEA had a friendly relationship with the government because of our mutual interest in combatting drug trafficking. I don't believe I was aware at the time that Senator McCain had been a POW in

Vietnam and had been tortured in the "Hanoi Hilton" for five plus years. I probably would have viewed our visit differently, but still I appreciated the two hours we had with him and I walked away with admiration and respect.

Watching his funeral on TV, being attended by many foreign dignitaries, I was moved by the numerous heartfelt eulogies delivered by many in our government, from all parties and persuasions, former presidents, and many people from all walks of life from around the world. It moved me to a sense of deep respect for his sacrifice and service and to a sober reflection on his life. Thank you for your service John McCain.

Separation and Change

As the time fast approached for my second tour in Burma to come to a close, my wife and kids prepared to return to Seattle in June. The timing of their relocation was important because she would appropriately attempt to get a teaching job in her former school district where she taught music at the elementary level in the fall. She did. They welcomed her back graciously. The DEA wished for me to stay on for an undetermined period of time because there was no one left to keep the lights on in our Country Office.

Kate and I had nothing that resembled a marital relationship of any kind any longer. It really was very clear to me and should have been to her also. I told her that after my open-ended extension in Burma, I would not be returning to our home. There wasn't much of a reaction in the moment but her wrath would manifest itself at a later time, which shocked even me, when the face of guile and rage revealed itself in full display. In the meantime, she drained our bank account. Being gullible at best or stupid, on the descending order of awareness, I didn't have a clue what was going on thousands of miles away. Maybe, at the time I didn't even care. "Hell, hath no fury like a woman scorned." If that was the price I had to pay, so be it.

Change is always a difficult thing to endure because through it we encounter the unknown which causes anxiety and even fear in extreme cases. Separation for me was not painful. It brought on a sense of relief because I was resolved in my decision and I was escaping the tortuous existence I had endured for the past 18 years. Staying in Burma for a few extra months was a blessing. There was security and familiarity of routine there. I had space to reflect and think. Any anxiety over change would not really be encountered until it was time to return to the States and start a new life. That's when real challenges would be faced. I was not relishing the idea of facing those challenges, but I had set sails to steer my ship into unchartered waters and look for new direction, in a new world. The Apostle Paul tells the Corinthians,

"We are always courageous for we walk by faith, not by sight." I don't know what my soon to be ex-wife was thinking but I had been unable to access any modicum of her thinking for some time, and largely gave up trying to do so.

The General and my Farewell

I remained in Burma for what ended up being six months due to the fact that there were no agents to manage the office except me because of an unfortunate incident which happened to the Country Attaché's wife. Patty had been involved in a rather nasty motor vehicle accident in Rangoon and badly damaged her hand. She would need surgery and extensive therapy, so they were forced to leave Burma prematurely, leaving me alone to man the office.

I did have a major project to deal with in the meantime, however. The Drug Czar, retired General Barry McCaffery, appointed to the Cabinet position by President Clinton, was coming to South East Asia to be briefed by the various relevant countries' DEA representatives about the overall drug situation and trafficking patterns in the region. I worked many hours in the days leading up to his visit putting together a briefing for him, which was complicated because of the complex history of conflict among the various ethnic groups in Burma as well as with the Government itself. I had help from an elderly gentleman who had worked many years within the Government and was somewhat of a student and expert on Burma's history. U Kin Maung put on his professor hat and gave me an in-depth tutorial on the subject.

Finally, the day arrived when I was to fly to Bangkok for the briefing, as the American Embassy there was the largest in the region. I felt very prepared and was looking forward to the delivery of my presentation. Prior to the briefing I had spent a couple of days in Rangoon with McCaffrey's assistant, Colonel Ralf Peters, talking to him about Burma and preparing for what to expect from the General. Colonel Peters is an extremely bright person who has authored books and made many appearances on television as an analyst on topics relating to foreign affairs. Spending time with him gave me confidence heading into the briefing with the Drug Czar.

When it was my turn to deliver my presentation, I stepped up to the podium, took out my notes and began. Several minutes into it I could sense that it was being well received by the General and everyone else in the room. While McCaffery had given other presenters a bit of a difficult time, peppering them with questions and interruptions, he seemed to just let me deliver my presentation without interruption, listening with interest to what I had to say. This began to give me more and more confidence in my performance and delivery. I was experiencing a growing sense of accomplishment as I pulled together the patch work of complexities in Burma's history with its ethnic groups and their economic concerns. About forty-five minutes into my talk, he asked a simple question: "Can we work with them?" The question, in that moment infused me with an overdose of enthusiasm juice and an un needed infusion of energy which throughout my life usually got me into trouble. His question was music to my ears.

The entire room broke out in laughter but I was too amped up to realize why. It was not until years later when I encountered one of the agents who had been in attendance at the time, in Los Angeles, did I learn the cause for the outbreak of laughter in the room that day. After all those years, when we met again, Brian laughed and said, "Dave that was very ballsy of you to ask General McCaffery if he was crazy." I was aghast and asked him if I really had said that. Well, I apparently had, and my time in Burma would soon come to an end. I hadn't been kicked out of the country, just replaced by a senior guy from DEA Headquarters. You don't ask a proud, retired General and Cabinet level official if he's crazy in front of a room full of people, at least not one with McCaffery's disposition. Colonel Peters had warned me that he could be difficult.

It was a super charged moment in the conference room at the Embassy in Bangkok that day, and it did in the end backfire on me personally, but maybe not in the larger pursuit of advancing U.S Government policy on Burma. A question like that being asked in a sincere, but rather abrupt way by the Drug Czar sent my energy level into hypersonic mode which didn't help my personal cause with him in the moment, but in the larger reality of international relationships, maybe I moved the needle. I guess in the moment I experienced a surge of adrenalin and momentarily lost my sense of who I was speaking to. That's small change though in the larger economy of things.

Burma was looked upon at the time as somewhat of a pariah by the United States Government, and the rest of the West, and I sensed this was a moment where I could make a definitive statement on the matter, and in doing so change US policy on its relationship with Burma. McCaffery's assistant, Colonel Peters strongly suggested to me after the briefing, that I "will have had a major impact" in shaping our relationship with Burma. In that ironic moment, it was a fair trade off.

A couple months later I would be leaving the sunny land of Burma, flying eastward over the Pacific Ocean headed for the dark and rainy, but familiar environs of Seattle. I was grateful for the nearly five years I spent there. The land and its culture would always hold a special place in my heart.

13

A Beauty to Rescue

A battle and adventure are not enough for a man. He yearns for romance. It's not enough to be the hero, he needs to be a hero to someone, in particular to the woman he loves. Things were just not right for Adam until God gave him Eve. I had never had romantic love in my heart for my ex-wife, only adolescent infatuation before we were married. I yearned for and sought that special kind of love that can make you want to be a hero and give your life for someone.

It was mid-December when we arrived in Seattle. It was quite a shock leaving the sunny, tropical climate of Burma and being greeted by the relatively dark, cold climate of Seattle in the winter. Additionally, the cold reality of finding a place to live and a divorce to finalize made it feel darker and colder than how the elements fairly deserved to be evaluated. The reason I use the plural form of the first person here, instead of "I" is because I had brought along with me my "Beauty" to rescue. I had a dilemma and a critical decision to make prior to leaving Burma. I really had found "my love" while there and faced the almost certain reality that if I didn't bring her out of the country when I still had the diplomatic juice to get her a passport and visa to the US, I most likely would never be able to. The Government was at the time still pretty closed and paranoid, and was not readily disposed to letting their treasure leave the country. This was my best and possibly only shot, and I had to make the audacious move at that time or never, so I reasoned.

While the time for our departure was quickly drawing near, she had still not received her Burmese passport. I was assured by my Military

Intelligence friends, whose help in the matter I sought and needed, that she would receive her passport before I was to leave for the States. Once the passport was in-hand, all I needed to do was secure a US visa for her, which I had already laid the groundwork for.

My Burmese counterpart friends came through at the last stressed filled minute and we were off to the US, together, with her father's blessing and well wishes. A new chapter in my life, unpredictable as it was, had dawned as the plane departed Rangoon, Burma on an eastward trek. New challenges and possibilities were in our future. I was in the hero and rescue mode, filled to the brim with purpose. I was ready to face any challenge or demon that I might encounter. I knew I would receive all kinds of resistance from family just based on how the picture looked, and I did, but I was up to the struggle with her by my side. What may have appeared to some as a fanciful folly transformed itself into life giving waters of grace that still flow in continuous cascading waves of joy after many years.

Now, what my grandmother had foretold when I was a young boy, that I would find the girl of my dreams, in the end came true. Thanks Grandma. I appreciate your prophetic words spoken to that young boy many years before, not comprehending what they meant . . . but you seemed to. You gave me the confidence and fortitude to face the appearance of scandal, even though I knew God's hand was in this then, and continues to be to this day.

Snowy Scene and Strange Sense of Surroundings

It was a dark, cloudy, windy, early morning when the Boeing 747 set down at SEATAC International Airport in Seattle, with winter fully on display. It was a shock to the system after leaving the warm, sunny tropics the day before, but I had a mission to carry out and couldn't afford to dwell on the comparisons. It was a monumental let down coming back to my former office to work after the exotic experience of working in a distant land and foreign culture with its complex historical and political issues to grapple with. In the States it was just the same old familiar crooks to outwit in the same familiar ways but that was reality in the moment. I had other much more pressing challenges to deal with, work issues becoming less an immediate preoccupation.

I found an apartment to rent not too far from my former home which my very soon to be ex-wife and children had moved back into. Actually, the separation proved to produce some very positive outcomes with regard to my relationship with my kids. Without having to constantly deal with the continuous dominating distraction of Kate's persona interfering with my parent-child interactions, some bright moments emerged amid the messy circumstances. We enjoyed some light hearted time together that thus far family dynamics had rarely allowed for. I attended my very talented daughter's high school track meets and hung out with her on the infields of the track in between her multiple pentathlon events, enjoying each other under the spring time sun. I took prolonged walks with my son through lush parkland gardens bordering regal Lake Washington, enjoying free-flowing undistracted conversations with him. They were rewarding moments that paid dividends more valuable than many hours of lessor quality of time spent within the insanely distractible environment formerly experienced in the same physical household with them. These were good and cherished moments, otherwise not realized.

All considered, there were some glimmers of light amid what most would consider a very negative outcome to a former marriage. God can, and will, turn all bad things to good if we choose to trust in him toward that end. We must trust with a cooperating spirit in his goodness. It's God's nature to steer all his creation toward that which is the good, with boundless love for all that his hand has made.

Financially I was running on fumes, and that might be putting too optimistic a spin on the situation. My emotional fumes were also quickly being consumed by the vitriolic flames being thrown my way. Times were a bit challenging under the circumstances but I was determined to march forward. Kate had wiped out my entire savings, leaving me with nothing, except my job which I was immensely grateful for. Out of desperation, after the required year back in the US working in a domestic office, I began to fantasize about landing another post overseas, in a warm weather, Third World country, where I might hope to regain my financial footing and at the same time rediscover some sorely missed sense of adventure again. I needed an injection of new scenery and a new adventure. I began searching for a place to satisfy both needs. I couldn't take the Seattle grey and gloom anymore, beautiful and green as it is. I had evolved into a sun being during my time in Burma. There had been an embryonic glimmer of a dream gestating in my mind which exploded into lively imaginative life one providential day, through the shadows of greyness which had been clouding my life; when my eyes fell upon a job announcement just posted. Color suddenly flashed into my colorless dream in a precious awakening to "possibility," painting a picture of what future life might look like. I felt the juices of excitement and potential begin to course through my constricted life veins once again. But I had by now learned that in life, impulse was not a prudent or reliable mentor. I had to sit on, think, and pray about this possibility for prosperity, meaning and purpose. It would be a gamble.

Sharp Turns and New Encounters

On that seemingly providential day, after having spent the minimal requisite time back in Seattle, I had been doing my daily due diligence of flipping through paper announcements for overseas job postings in hopes of finding a golden nugget. Seeing one that piqued my interest, and one that might possibly produce fruitful career outcomes, as well as practical needs, I pondered the possibility. While not exactly striking gold, maybe, at least, I had discovered a bit of tarnished brass that could be polished up, and work its way into my golden plan. The office in Port-au-Prince, Haiti was more than doubling its Special Agent personnel in reaction to Haiti's sudden emergence as a major transshipment country for cocaine coming from Colombia, then finding its way into the US. It was definitely considered a "hardship" post but, just as important to me, it was also in the sun soaked, blue water paradise of the Caribbean. Just what I needed in the moment!

I put in for the position, and not very much to my surprise, was selected with minimal political arm twisting needed. No revelation here given the nature of the place. Having overseas experience definitely gave me an advantage, although seeking to go to Haiti was probably more of a desperation move on my part than a romantic one. Either way, I was about to embark on another adventure that, although sincere about the job and its challenges, concomitantly thought it could be a bit rough and a trying one. I wasn't wrong in judgment on that front. There is some wisdom and truth to the saying, "be careful what you wish for," but fast closing in, was desperation on the financial front, and I badly needed an escape from the current, cataclysmic panorama I saw in my futuristic looking vision. I was eager to take the shot and the gamble. There are some situations that sometimes demand risk embracing approaches to life and this seemed fittingly to fall into that category quite neatly. I was off to language school in Arlington, Virginia to study French and Haitian Creole, requirements for the assignment in Haiti. The divorce was behind me, a new path before me, and I had a pocketful of faith and trust in God to guide me. I would need it.

New Life in Treacherous Terrain

I married my "beauty" from Burma, the girl of my dreams, in an Arlington, Virginia court house. Sweet's brother Soe Myint was our witness. It was a Friday morning and immediately after the rather simple ceremony we drove down to Bryson City, North Carolina where my brother has a home on beautiful Lake Fontana in the Smokey Mountains as sort of a weekend honeymoon to codify and celebrate our wedding. We were received warmly by my brother and his loving wife. They had left for us as a welcome gesture, a basket of cheese and assorted snacks along with a bottle of nice wine, placed decoratively in the small room at the quaint, rustic resort where we had arranged to stay after our rather late evening arrival. It wasn't a wedding banquet, but it placed a positive stamp on our humble, yet momentous celebration of love for each other and was a nice symbolic endorsement of our declaration and official leap into a new life of commitment. A simple but warm symbol of acceptance and approval, capping off the auspicious day.

It was just a three-day trip but with their warm acceptance and affirmation it felt like we had experienced a regal wedding and memorable honeymoon. We did. It's amazing how simple but positive affirmation can transform a simple experience into something very special and unforgettable. They left a lasting impression that is with me to this day, more than 20 years later.

We spent nearly eight months in Virginia with me doing my best to learn the two languages. I did well enough to pass and got the green light to go to Haiti. Appropriately, my teacher was Haitian so I also received a bit of cultural indoctrination in addition to learning the dialect. I was taking my new bride on a five-year honeymoon to Haiti, although at the time I had no clue of the duration. "Hardship tours" are normally two years. Bringing my bride to Haiti might have been cause for certain and swift divorce in many cases, but sweet as she is, Sweet is also a trooper with the will and fortitude as hard and strong as steel. She thrived in Haiti. Sweet is the name her father gave her, Sweet Sweet Lone to be precise. Very unorthodox for Burmese names but her father named her after an American diplomat, who's name sounded to him like Sweetlone, and in who's car she was delivered while driving her mom to the hospital in the middle of the night, on Valentine's Day no less.

Typical Burmese names go something like: Win Win Htay, Sweet's sister's name, or Toe Aung Htay, or Aung Lin Htut. There are no sur names or family last names, but names to which some meaning is attached. They're descriptive. I was given a Burmese name by a language teacher I worked with for a while in Burma; Ko Pyon Cho, which means "Sweet Smile," the "Ko" part of the name is simply a relational moniker for brother or something of an equal in terms of age and status. An older male, in a show of respect begins with "U" as in Mr., or Uncle, a woman by "Daw," which roughly translates to Aunt. A strange way of naming people to us in the West, but very ancient and sensibly appropriate to that culture.

Pots and Pans Sending a Message

I had an unforgettable paranormal-like experience while still in Arlington, VA, toward the end of language school. Since early childhood I had always been very close to my mom's brother, my Uncle Jack, who I introduced earlier as being a mentor and someone very dear to me. There seemed to be a kind of chemistry between us that is not often experienced in human relationships, at least it felt like that to me. Although certainly not unique, it was something to cherish, and I did. He was now dying of lung cancer in his western North Carolina home in the mountains. I had recently written him a letter having a sort of farewell ring to it, in which I told him that when he goes to his heavenly place to take me with him, meaning; don't forget me when departing this world. He wrote back saying that he would definitely rattle some pots and pans to let me know what he's up to. One early March morning a few minutes past five o'clock, I was literally jolted out of my sleep and thrown from my bed. It felt like some sort of electric shock with a force that launched me into the air and onto the floor, ultimately landing gently on the soft plush carpet. I was not hurt in any way. When I spoke to his wife, Marsha later that day, she informed me that Jack had passed away just past five o'clock in the morning. He did more than rattle a few pots and pans. He airmailed me a personal message, in no subtle way, that he was, in the moment, leaving this world. He came through on his promise in typical dramatic humor. That was his final farewell to me and an indelible reminder that he would remain near, watching over things. I appreciated the sudden wakeup call and reminder, to remain always in a ready posture for the reality of mysteries that lay beyond our grasp or understanding. Stay awake and alert for that which is unseen.

Language school completed, we drove back across the country from D.C. to Seattle with stops in Milwaukee and Minneapolis to visit family and friends. Unfortunately, instead of the logical, smooth transfer to the foreign country whose language I had toiled to learn in the preceding eight months; I languished in Seattle for almost a year because of some funding hiccups in Washington. "Use it or lose it" was applicable to my newly acquired, yet tenuous language abilities; still in their infantile developmental launch, fading rapidly on their way to the "lost and found," finally landing in the lost bin after too many months in mothballs. Funding for the transfer eventually got worked out and we were on our way. The heck with French and Haitian Creole. I would wing it and make people understand me somehow, and I would understand them in return.

PART III

Change, Challenge, and Conquest

14

Suffering Haiti, A History and Culture of Discord

As we approached the Haitian coast line on our temporary orientation trip there, I looked out the left side window of the American Airlines, Boeing 747 as it descended in its slow, lumbering fashion. I was in awe, staring at the display of natural beauty and blend of brilliant, blue, Caribbean water, meeting the cinematic view of the mountainous terrain and coast line in its splendid welcome. The beauty defied the enigmatic land it veiled in its mirage. The brilliant water seemed to reflect God's beauty in creation, and it caught me in a riveting moment of grace-filled wonder as I took in the majestic view. The momentary reflection instantly turned into a contemplative one for several unregistered moments. Looking down on the poorest nation in the western Hemisphere from above, the scene belied its reality. It was beautiful from that lofty dimension, natural beauty in its intended form seen from far away, but poverty and abuse of the land rooted in the Haitian people's suffering history of oppression, slavery, and pervasive corruption drove the land into its impoverished sad state. Abuse of the people resulted in reciprocal treatment of the land and environment, leaving it baron and crying out for care, in need of some serious nurturing stewardship. On the ground, it looked a mess and in stark contrast to what I observed from on high. Once on the ground, the case was made that the Country was deserving of its lowly, poorest nation in the hemisphere status.

The initial drive from the airport to the hotel in the more upscale city of Petionville was not too indicative of the country's impoverished status.

The route we were taken on was a diversion from the reality of the prevailing poverty of the country. I was somewhat saddened at the sight of the abject poverty and barrenness of this country after a more eye-opening opportunity to observe the place over the ensuing days. Over the two centuries of foreign occupation and slavery, the struggle for independence was finally won by the former slaves, but it resulted in abuse of the land. Snatched from the indigenous people by colonial, imperial adventurers, Haiti was ultimately taken over by the liberators of slavery, former slaves themselves. But in its evolution, the land was eventually stripped of its trees as they were cut down and used to make charcoal for cooking, creating a bad recipe for all who ate at the table.

It is a sad sight to lay eyes upon when the effects consistently turn deadly on a yearly basis when the monsoon rains faithfully return each summer, leaving the lower elevations of the country and its inhabitants buried in mountains of mud. Haiti, a mountainous country, experiences heavy tropical rains which cause giant mud slides that invariably kill many people each year because of deforestation. It was so unlike the lush foliage throughout Burma, also a third world country, but the people there seem to have been better caretakers of the land and its natural beauty. I felt a sudden pang of nostalgia for Burma upon my arrival in Haiti but I bucked up for whatever the tasks were that lay ahead. Burma was in the past and I had only the present to deal with. This was my commitment now and however forlorn the place looked, I was going to make it work, although, little did I foresee just what a challenge that was going to be at first glance.

The Haitian people generally talk at a level of volume that far exceeds what is needed for normal communication, probably an expressive way of communication telling of something more than just the words that convey a message. Something on a humanly deeper level. This was so much in contrast to how the Burmese people speak in respectful, much quieter tones, and was something I had to adjust to. Although I am not a student on the subject of language, the differences are probably a cultural derivative of their anthropology. I told myself I had to quit making comparisons and surrender to the reality of the current environment and culture. Haitians in general are very expressive and fun-loving people in spite of the squalor that surrounds them. We settled in and grew used to our new, yet sometimes shocking surroundings.

Diplomats did not have it so bad as there is a wealthy class of people in Haiti who own many nice houses which are rented out to diplomats and adventurous foreign business people.

Street name signs are scarce in the city of Port-au-Prince, so when we settled into a house on the outskirts of the city, after our official transfer there, I initially had to use landmarks to mark the turns required to navigate my way to the Embassy, which was located in the downtown area of Port-au-Prince; and locate them again on the return commute home. One laughable marker I used initially was at an intersection where I needed to make a turn to venture up the steep hill to our residence. It was a small mountain of garbage with a resident, very large pig typically rummaging through it. It provided a chuckle each time I passed by it to and from the Embassy. The heap of garbage and its pig fortunately remained a fixture there long enough for me to become sufficiently acclimated to the area. Garbage collection in the city is not a smooth and regular function of the local government. So, the pig in the garbage was a blessing for a while and served a purpose, in addition to providing some entertainment. Haiti as a country has its own character and place in the world-wide scheme of things and I'm sure has its own unique purpose in the Creator's design, even though it may not be readily apparent to us in the moment.

It was not unusual to see a dead body lying in the street when driving around the streets of Port-au-Prince. They would not be removed immediately because of some silly sounding law which required the Medical Examiner to come and personally pronounce the dead, dead and remove the corpse. Kind of an unsanitary and undignified practice, I thought.

Haiti's history of corruption is most assuredly a central reason for its poverty as there has always been a ruling class since it won its independence in 1804, that has always looked out for its own interests with little regard for the welfare of the country and its people. When Jean Bertrand Aristide first came to power in 1990, a former priest who had risen up from the common class, there was great hope for change. He was a champion of the common people when he appeared on the political scene, but sadly, corruption continued to flourish blatantly under his presidential leadership and direction. Corruption is built into the genetic makeup of the political culture and has been the defining thread in the country's fabric since its embryonic beginnings. A brief look at Haiti's sordid, tortured history is suggested here to put into clearer perspective and relevance, why and ultimately how my experience and story came to be, at that particular time in the country's history. Just one small, tiny parcel in time in a long succession of Haiti's troubled chapters of governance. But this time was mine to live in, to own, and to influence . . . with some help from the Director, as always seems to be the case.

A Tale of Terror and Tears into Troubled Independence

When Christopher Columbus happened upon a large island in the Western Atlantic, now known as the Caribbean, in 1492, it was inhabited by the indigenous Taino and Arawakan people. He immediately claimed the island for the Spanish Crown naming it La Isla Espanola ("The Spanish Island"), later known as Hispaniola. French influence began to appear in 1625 and French control of the western third of the Island fully emerged in 1660 which came to be known as Saint-Domingue, modern day Haiti. It became one of France's wealthiest colonies, producing large quantities sugar and coffee on the backs of a brutal slave system. Inspired by the message of the French Revolution, Haitian slaves rose up in revolt against the French in 1791. Tradition marks the beginning of the revolution at a voodoo ceremony held on August 14, 1791, in the northern region of the colony near what is now known as Cap-Haitian. The call to arms was issued by a voodoo priest by the name of *Dutty Boukman*, and within hours plantations in the area were in flames and the rebellion quickly spread throughout the entire colony. Boukman was captured and executed, but the rebellion continued to rapidly gain momentum and intensity.

Toussaint Louverture and his corps of battle-hardened former slaves got word that in France slavery had been abolished and emancipation won. They joined with the French Republican movement in May 1794. There was internecine fighting between former slaves under Toussaint and groups of mulatto strongholds, but eventually Toussaint prevailed and by 1801, he had control over all of Hispaniola including Spanish controlled Santo Domingo which he had also conquered. Toussaint did not seek retribution against the former slaveholders believing that the French on the island were not inclined to reinstate slavery. He did, however, assert so much independence that Napoleon sent a massive force from France under the command of his brother-in-law Charles Leclerc, to reinstate French control and restore slavery. Toussaint was duped by Leclerc, arrested and sent off to France to die in Prison.

Two of Toussaint's former lieutenants, *Jacques Jean (J.J.) Dessalines and Henry Christophe*, as well as the leader of the mulatto forces, *Alexander Petion*, had transferred their allegiance to the French but after seeing what Leclerc had done to Toussaint, these commanders along with others once again resumed to battle against Leclerc and the French forces under him. With the French intent on reconquest and re-enslavement of the colony's black population, the war intensified with one bloody atrocity after another. The rainy season brought with it, yellow fever and malaria which took a heavy toll on the French soldiers. The disease caused 24,000 deaths and another 8,000 soldiers being hospitalized, in addition to leaving Leclerc a casualty of the disease.

Napoleon replaced Leclerc with *Donatien-Marie-Joseph de Vimeur Rochambeau*. Rochambeau wrote Napoleon a letter which informed him that in order to reclaim the colony, France must declare the former black slaves, slaves again. Additionally, he would need to annihilate 30,000 men and women to subdue the former slaves and ensure his victory. In his desperation, Rochambeau repeatedly turned to despicable acts of brutality. A passage from Henri Christophe's personal secretary, himself a former slave, describes the horrible atrocities inflicted on them by their French oppressors under Rochambeau.

> "Have they not hung-up men with heads downward, drowned them in sacks, crucified them on planks, buried them alive, crushed them in mortars? Have they not forced them to eat excrement? And, having flayed them with the lash, have they not cast them alive to be devoured by worms, or onto anthills, or lashed them to stakes in the swamp to be devoured by mosquitoes? Have they not thrown them into boiling cauldrons of cane syrup? Have they not put men and women inside barrels stubbed with spikes and rolled them down mountainsides into the abyss? Have they not consigned these miserable blacks to man-eating dogs until the later, sated by human flesh, left the mangled victims to be finished off with bayonet and poniard?"[1]

In 1803 France returned to war with Britain. With the Royal Navy firmly in control of the seas, reinforcements and supplies for Rochambeau never arrived in sufficient numbers. The tide turned toward the former slaves and Napoleon eventually abandoned his dreams of restoring France's New World empire. With France's concentration turned to its war with Britain and Europe, and the devastation the French army suffered at the Battle of Vertieres at the hands of the British on November, 1803, independence by the former slaves of Hispaniola was won. On January 1, 1804, Dessalines declared Haiti's independence from France, officially becoming the independent Republic of Haiti.

Unlike Toussaint, Dessalines showed little equanimity toward the oppressors. In a final act of retribution, the remaining French were slaughtered by Haitian military forces leaving some 2,000 expatriates massacred at Cap-Haitian in the North, 900 in Port-au-Prince, and 400 at Jeremy, in the southern coastal area of the country. He issued a proclamation declaring: "We have repaid these cannibals, war for war, crime for crime, outrage for outrage."

1. "History of Haiti."

Thus, Haiti became the first black republic and the oldest democratic republic in the Western Hemisphere. The nation of former slaves was, however, excluded from the hemisphere's first regional meeting of independent nations held in Panama in 1826. Furthermore, owing to entrenched opposition from Southern slave states in the U.S., Haiti did not receive U.S. diplomatic recognition until 1862, after the South ceded from the Union and the war over slavery was on in the fractured United States of America.

Continuing Succession of Chaos and Corruption

Since winning independence Haiti has had a troubled history of chaotic and tumultuous governance and leadership successions almost continuously throughout its history. After achieving its autonomy, many of those transfers of power involved Coup d'états and strong-arm tactics, favored arrangements, or necessary ones in its ongoing progression of messy transfers of leadership. Peaceful transitions of power have been the exception in Haiti's story of independence.

On September 22, 1804, Dessalines, preferring Napoleon's style of rule, declared himself Emperor Jacques I. His empire ended badly though, when two of his advisors, *Henri Christophe* and *Alexandre Petion*, contrived his assassination on October 17, 1806, north of Port-au-Prince, while he was in route to do battle with rebels fighting against his regime. After the coup d'état, these two central conspirators divided the country into competing regimes. Christophe created the authoritarian State of Haiti in the North, proclaiming himself King Henri I, while Petion established the Republic of Haiti in the South. While Petion's government was always on the brink of bankruptcy, it produced one of the most liberal and tolerant Haitian governments in the country's history.

In 1816, however, finding the burden of the Senate intolerable, Petion suspended the legislature and declared his office of President to be one for life, which did not last long for him because he died of yellow fever shortly thereafter. His assistant *Jean-Pierre Boyer* replaced him.

In the North, Christoph established a nobility class fashioning society after Europe's monarchies. In 1820, however, weakened by illness and waning support for his authoritarian regime, Christoph killed himself with a silver bullet rather than face a coup d'état. Boyer then was successful in reuniting Haiti through diplomacy and served as president until his overthrow. Haiti's early years were off to a tumultuous beginning and were emblematic of what would characterize much of its history up to and into the modern era.

Boyer was overthrown in a revolt led by *Charles Riviere-Herard* in 1843, when he, for a brief time established parliamentary rule under the Constitution of 1843. It was not long after, however, that revolts broke out throughout the country and chaos descended on Haiti once again. There were several transient, strongman presidents who ruled harshly until 1847 when *General Faustin Soulouque*, a former slave who fought for Haiti's independence became president. He purged the military of its high command, established secret police, and eliminated his opponents. In 1849 he unabashedly proclaimed himself to be Haiti's second emperor, Faustin I Soulouque. He was led to invade the Dominican Republic by his conviction that the white and mulatto rulers there were his natural enemies and he believed he would not consolidate his power until he dominated the whole Island of Hispaniola. His first foray into the Spanish speaking country took place shortly after proclaiming himself emperor. Dominican President Buenaventura Baez, in return declared war on Haiti. Soulouques' second attempted excursion into the Dominican Republic was met with horrific resistance and ultimate defeat when at the Haitian border town of Quanaminthe, In January 1856, his contingent of 6,000 soldiers were soundly crushed. More than 1,000 were killed, many more were wounded or declared missing on their way back to the capital city of Port-au-Prince. When Soulouque arrived at the capital with what remained of his largely diminished army he was cursed by many women who had lost their husbands, brothers, and sons. Soulouque's image was badly damaged. Four years later he was deposed by *General Fabre Geffrard*.

Geffrard's military government remained in power until 1867, while he promoted a successful policy of national reconciliation. In 1860, he reached an agreement with the Vatican in Rome, reintroducing Roman Catholic institutions in Haiti, which included Catholic schools. An attempt was also made in 1867 to establish a constitutional government, but the subsequent president *Sylvain Salnave* was overthrown in 1869 and following him, *Nissage Saget*, experienced the same fate in 1874. A workable constitution was formed under *Michel Domingue* and a relatively prolonged period of democratic peace and development ensued. Uncharacteristically, in 1879, Michel Domingue's government peacefully transferred power to *Lysius Salomon* for the first time in the country's young history. Salomon is recorded in the county's annuls as having been an able and capable leader.

Haiti reached a benchmark during this period where monetary reform and cultural renaissance blossomed, and Haitian art flourished. The last decades of the nineteenth century ushered in an era of intellectual culture. Major works of history were published and intellectuals led by Louis-Joseph Janvier and Anenor Firmin engaged in discourses challenging the growing tide of racism and social Darwinism emerging at the time. Haiti flourished, largely due to the positive influence of the Constitution of 1867, which did much to improve overall stability, the economy, and well-being of the nation and its people. The functional Constitution had much influence on inspiring confidence in legal systems and restoring faith in them among the Haitian people. This period of prosperity ended abruptly in 1911 when revolution again broke out and Haiti was once again thrown back into its more characteristic mode of disorder and subsequent dept.

Between 1911 and 1915, there were six different presidents, each of whom was either assassinated or driven into exile. Revolutionary armies emerged throughout the country, made up of peasant brigands, recruited by rival political factions who made promises of monetary compensation after successful raids on opposing factions and were promised the opportunity to plunder the conquered. In February 1915, *Vilbrun Guillaume Sam* declared himself the country's ruler and dictator. In July, facing another revolt he massacred 167 political prisoners, all of whom were from elite families, and he was, not surprisingly, subsequently lynched by an outraged mob in Port-au-Prince. The country had quickly devolved from its promising pinnacle of development and had fallen back into its sad but all too familiar pattern of unrest and violence . . . a tortured history indeed. Can this cycle of de-evolution into chronic dysfunction be broken? One has to ask the question.

The German community in Haiti had seemed more at ease with integrating into Haitian society than other foreign groups, especially the French, and married into the wealthier mulatto families. They were the primary financiers for the numerable revolutions, providing high interest rate loans to the various competing political factions. In an effort to curb German influence and the resultant political chaos, the U.S. State Department backed a consortium of American investors, under the leadership of the National City Bank of New York, and acquired control of the Haitian government's treasury as well as the *Banque Nationale d'Haiti*, the nation's only commercial bank. The concerned parental neighbor to the north, recognized the abhorrent behavior of the troubled child to the south, and saw a crisis in the region that needed immediate tough love. Order in the neighborhood was urgently called for, behavioral correction was needed, and that judgment compelled parental discipline to be swiftly applied. The United States could not tolerate out of control chaos in the region and swiftly moved to intervene.

United States Occupation

In response to the complaints by American banks, to whom Haiti was deeply in dept, President Woodrow Wilson sent an occupation force to Haiti in 1915, which was widely resented by Haitians due to their loss of sovereignty. Not surprisingly, revolts sprang up against the American forces, but reforms did take place and stability was restored in spite of hurt feelings and adolescent rebellion.

Under the supervision of the U.S. Marines, *Philippe Sudre Dartiguenave* was elected president by the Haitian National Assembly. He signed a treaty that made Haiti a *de jure* US protectorate, with American officials assuming control and supervision over Haiti's Financial Adviserership, Customs Receivership, the Constabulary, the Public Works Service, and the Public Health Service. This oversight and control lasted for ten years. The primary instrument for enforcing American authority was the newly created *Gendarmerie d' Haiti* (military style police) commanded by American officers.

A new constitution was written, largely authored by the U.S. State Department and the Department of the Navy. Under Harry Truman's presidency, Franklin D. Roosevelt, Under Secretary for the Navy at the time, claimed to have personally written the constitutional document. At the urging of American officials, a decision was made to dissolve the Haitian National Assembly when it refused to approve the document and the body was forcibly dissolved by the *Gendarmerie*. The constitution then was passed by a plebiscite in 1919, in which less than five percent of the people voted, and of that contingent 97% were illiterate, in most cases ignorant of what they were voting for as well. It was, however, approved by the State Department.

The US Marines and the *Gendarmerie* initiated an extensive road building project to enhance their military effectiveness and open the country to increased US investment. Construction was largely carried out by unpaid conscripted peasant labor, in lieu of paying road taxes, a tricky law that the French employed when peasant labor was used by their Feudal Lords. By 1918, more than 470 miles of roads had been built and repaired, including a road linking Port-au-Prince to Cap Haitian in the most northern part of the country, on the coast. (I travelled this same road several times when in Haiti and am quite sure no maintenance had been done on the road's surface since it was built in 1918. The drive was always a brutal endeavor, as well as dangerous.) Haitians forced to work in the labor-gangs, often dragged from their homes by armed guards, received little benefit from these improvements and viewed the forced labor a return to slavery at the hands of white men.

In 1919, a new uprising sprung up from disillusioned peasants. Led by *Charlemagne Peralte*, who vowed to drive the occupiers into the sea and liberate Haiti once again, the rebels attacked Port-au-Prince but were driven back, suffering heavy casualties in the process. Subsequently, a creole speaking American Gendarmerie officer and two US Marines infiltrated Peralte's camp, killed him and photographed his corpse in an attempt to demoralize the rebels. *Benoit Batraville* succeeded Peralte and launched another assault on the capital. His death in 1920, marked the end of the rebellion. In 1921, the Marine Corps Commandant reported to the US Senate during hearings that during the nearly two years of resistance, 2,250 Haitians had been killed. In a report to the Secretary of the Navy, however, he reported that 3,250 had been killed. Haitian historians estimate the number as being much higher, one suggesting that somewhere in the neighborhood of 15,000 may have perished during the pacification period.

During the ensuing regime under *Louis Borneo*, who ruled without a legislature, Haiti returned to economic expansion and its infrastructure was vastly improved and expanded. Herbert Hoover appointed two commissions to Haiti in the wake of ten Haitians being killed by marines in Les Cayes during a protest over poor economic conditions in 1929. *Stenio Vincent*, a long-time critic of the occupation was elected president in a fully democratic election in 1934. He instituted a new kind of military force known as the *Guard* which kept internal order while supporting a popularly elected government. In theory it was apolitical, although in practice, those types of arrangements never are. The U.S. military began to leave Haiti shortly thereafter, and by 1934, it had departed the country entirely.

Vincent, however, had acquired full authority over economic matters, having been transferred from the legislature to the executive branch. He also reorganized the judiciary in his efforts to amass more power. Vincent governed largely to benefit himself and a clique of his cronies as well as a handful of corrupt military officers. An attempted coup by *Guard* military officers led Vincent to purge the *Guard* officer corps of all members suspected of being disloyal, marking the end of an "apolitical" military. He attempted to stay in power a third term but the United States under the Roosevelt administration made it quite clear that it would not tolerate a third term for Vincent and he subsequently acquiesced and relinquished power to *Eli Lescot*.

15

The Early Modern Era

Lescot was a government bureaucrat who many considered to be a well-qualified candidate for the presidency but like the majority of his Haitian predecessors, failed to live up to his potential in his lust and grab for more power. He suppressed opponents, censored the press, and compelled the legislature to grant him extensive power, ignoring their place in the proper order of democratic governance. Lescot's misuse and abuse of power eventually led to strikes and protests by students, government workers, teachers, and shopkeepers throughout Haiti. His mulatto-dominated, class rule also alienated the predominantly black Haitian *Guard* making his position untenable which ultimately led to his resignation in January, 1946. With the sudden power vacuum created by his abdication, the *Guard* assumed power and would govern by way of a three-member military junta.

The junta made a pledge to hold free elections in the near future but lacking in any clear knowledge as to how to make the transition, it dragged its feet until public clamor and demonstrations forced them to make good on their promise. Haiti elected a National Assembly in May, 1946, and then set a date of August 16, 1946, when it would select a president. *Dumarsais Estime* was a former school teacher and cabinet minister who was viewed as the most stable of the three contenders, one of whom was a twenty-six-year-old and the other a member of the Communist party. Estime was elected by the Assembly to be most suited to hold the office among the three. He was a civilian of humble origins and was passionately anti-elitist, which translates to generally mean, being anti-mulatto. He was successful in expanding the school system, raising the salaries of government workers, and elevating the representation of middle and lower-class blacks. He also attempted to curry favor with the Haitian *Guard* which had been renamed the Haitian Army.

Estime, however, fell victim to the seemingly unavoidable, time-proven pitfalls of Haitian rulers: elite intrigue, personal power, and ambition, clearly a common characteristic throughout Haiti's political and ruling class history. He alienated the elite class by blocking them from any governmental positions of importance and horrified the Europeanized elite by proposing that the practice of Voodoo be elevated as a religion to be on par with Roman Catholicism, which had been brought to the country by the French and Spanish. He also attempted to manipulate the constitution in order to extend his term in office. The elite class, having no influence in Haitian governmental affairs because of his policies, covertly conspired with the Army officer corps, and on May 5, 1950, Estime was forced into resignation by the army. He was escorted from the Palace and sent into exile to Jamaica. The same three-person junta who assumed power before Estime's election re-emerged and once again took control of the government.

Free elections were again planned and on October 8, 1950, *Magloire*, a key figure in Estime's overthrow, resigned from the junta and declared himself a candidate for the presidency. The populace now understood implicitly that only a strong candidate, with both the military and elite class backing, would be best suited as a candidate to assume power. Magloire had minimal competition and was elected and seated as president on December 6, 1950. He re-established the elite to prominence. Although Magloire jailed political opponents and shut down their presses he was not overly harsh, but following in the footsteps of many of his predecessors he ignored the termination date of his tenure. Corruption rose to a magnitude not seen in Haiti before, to the disillusionment of almost all Haitians. People took to the streets in protest of his failure to step down. While he declared martial law, a general strike shutting down the Capitol forced him to resign. Like his predecessor, Magloire was forced to flee to Jamaica in May, 1956, and the army was again left to restore order.

The two-year period between Magloire's ouster and the election of *Francois Duvalier (Papa Doc)*, in 1957, proved to be a particularly chaotic time for Haiti, even by typical, dysfunctional Haitian standards. Three provisional presidents held the office in just those two short, unstable years. One resigned and the army unceremoniously deposed the other two.

Duvalier, A More Horrific Face of Dictator

A former Minister of Health, Francois Duvalier had earned the reputation as being a humanitarian during his ascension in the political world, but took little time in establishing yet another dictatorship, regarded as one of the most repressive and corrupt of all Haitian power grabs in the modern era. Combining violence with the dark superstitions and insidious exploitations of Voodoo spirituality, Duvalier instilled fear into the hearts of the Haitian population and political opponents. His paramilitary Volunteers for National Security, more commonly known as the *Tonton Macoute*, were named after a mythical Voodoo monster. His terrifying security apparatus routinely carried out political murders, beatings and oppressive intimidation on any potential threat to his grip on power among the populace or anyone else who he perceived to harbor any inkling of not bending to his authority. Rape was ritualistically and routinely employed as a political tool to silence opposition among the domestic population. It is estimated that 30,000 Haitians were killed by Duvalier's villainous, heinous, intimidation machine. He incorporated "Houngans," Voodoo priests, into the ranks of the *Macoute* giving his official approval and recognition to Voodoo practice and its Houngan practitioners. By endorsing and bestowing "official" status on *Tonton Macoute,* Duvalier normalized Voodoo into Haiti's religious, cultural, and political affairs. In short, Duvalier quickly and violently restructured Haiti's social, political, and spiritual psyche.

Duvalier was devoted to his private adherence to the practice of Voodoo and was reputed to have personal knowledge and credible mastery of magic and sorcery. His embrace of Voodoo practice and his personal powers in the dark realm strangely enhanced his persona among the common people, and oddly increased his legitimacy as a political leader among them. (I, not so strangely, wonder if this kind of indoctrination and embrace of Satanic influence into a culture and country does not have a degrading and devasting impact on its functioning capacity. A theory to be considered, social science theorists.)

Duvalier's policies were designed to end the dominance of the elite class and their political influence. His policies and war with the elite class led to the emigration of many educated Haitians, exacerbating the country's economic and social problems to new levels. Duvalier appealed to some of the middle class by providing infrastructure projects to neighborhoods in need of paved roads, running water, and sewage systems. The Kennedy Administration suspended aid to Haiti in 1961, after allegations surfaced that Duvalier was pocketing much of the aid money sent to the country by the U.S., and was secretly planning to use a U.S. Marine Corps aid mission in

Haiti to further strengthen the *Macoute*. In 1964 Duvalier declared himself president for life and remained so until he died in 1971.

Baby Doc (1971–86)

Upon Duvalier's death, power was passed onto his son, 19-year-old *Jean-Claude Duvalier (Baby Doc)*. Even though he discontinued some of his father's more terrifying and oppressive political tactics, Haiti's economy and political system continued to steadily decline even more. This occurred despite the fact that foreign governments were more tolerant and benevolent toward the son and were offering more assistance in aid. Jean-Claude was fairly inept at governing, or in any administrative ability for that matter, largely leaving those mundane tasks to his mother, Simone Duvalier. Jean-Claude preferred to expend much of his energies living the life of a playboy and amassing a fortune through fraudulent and corrupt schemes that amounted to hundreds of millions of dollars over the years. He married a beautiful divorcee, Michele Bennet, in a three-million-dollar wedding ceremony that left many Haitians aghast and disillusioned. Jean-Claude's style was starkly in contrast to his father's more conservative image and his strict adherence of loyalty to the black middle class. His new bride convinced Jean-Claude to ostracize his mother Simone, and she was subsequently forced to leave Haiti.

With the country in rapid decline and the outbreak of African Swine flu and AIDS, discontent with Jean-Claude grew to pitch levels after Pope John Paul II condemned the regime in the wake of a visit to Haiti in 1983. Once again, consistent with their tumultuous and calamitous history, rebellion broke out. After months of disorder and chaos, Jean-Claud Duvalier was forced by the army to resign and into exile in February, 1986.

From 1986 until early 1988, Haiti was once again ruled by a provisional military government under *General Namphy*. A new constitution was ratified and both local and national elections were scheduled for November, 1987, but were cancelled when the military was alleged to have planned the massacre of up to 300 hundred would be voters on election day. Military leaders who either orchestrated or condoned the massacre quickly moved in to cancel the elections and retake control of the Government. Presidential elections were again scheduled several months later but most of the candidates who had run for president previously, did not attempt to do so the second time around. Professor *Leslie Manigat* was elected in 1988 with only four percent of the population turning out to vote. Instability remained as the soup du jure, as did many politically motivated killings.

John Bosco Massacre and Rise of Jean-Bertrand Aristide

A significant event took place on September 11, 1988, in Port-au-Prince. Remembered as the John Bosco Massacre, when the Catholic church was attacked and a reported 13 to 50 people were killed with some 80 injured during the three-hour long assault. The church itself was burned to the ground. Parish priest, later turned politician, Jean-Bertrand Aristide, up to that point, had already been the target of several assassination attempts for his outspoken anti-Duvalier rhetoric and his political preaching from the pulpit. A Roman Catholic priest of the Salesian Order, Aristide was an adherent of liberation theology. His philosophy and unreserved public proclamations, strongly critical of any sort of authoritarian control, was an existential threat to the status quo of those in Haiti's progression of power brokers and their brutal means of control. Aristide dared to speak out against it loudly and publicly. Therefore, he became a target of the powerful, but was also emerging as a champion of the oppressed and the poor, an overabundance of those in supply at the time, as is the case all the time.

The attack on John Bosco Catholic Church was carried out by unidentified armed men who may have been former *Tonton Macoute*, as is the suspicion. The secret police and the powerful, would naturally be averse to any kind of evangelical liberation theology, as their inclinations were more closely aligned with brutal acts, the sacraments of their religion of control.

The John Bosco Massacre was carried out with no interference whatsoever being provided by the police or military, both of whom were available to intervene but chose to do nothing. The Mayor of Port-au-Prince at the time, Frank Romain, a former leader of the *Tonton Macoute*, was accused of being involved, and was reported to have said after the attack that Aristide had been "justly punished." The intimidation tactics did not have the desired effect on the priest, however. On the contrary, Aristide's quick assent to fame and power as champion of the oppressed and the poor, turned ruling class heads in startling fashion, although the hierarchy of the Catholic Church in Rome was far from impressed. The Catholic Church was losing patience with Aristide's left turn to radical political interests; away from his official responsibility as priest, to Sheppard his people by way of the Gospel, the central vision of the Church. Aristide had moved away from that centrality toward radical political passions and therefore moved the Church hierarchy to a place where they had no reasonable, acceptable place for him in the context of its mission in the world. His preaching had turned political and Aristide's radical liberation theology and message, looking more like political ambitions for himself, could no longer hold a proper place in the *Holy Order* of things.

A Serpent Slithers In

Coincidentally, in that confluence of discord and dysfunction, the ripe environmental mixture for opportunity presented itself as the vulnerable country caught the attention of the opportunistic Colombian cocaine trafficker, Pablo Escobar. He quickly swooped in to co-opt key components within the country's security institutions to advance his massive trafficking enterprise. He had already lured top Haitian officials into his pocket with little effort. Most likely, those who were caught in that web, were not fans of Aristide. A lot of moving parts and unpredictable dynamics were in play at the time, but one dominant theme always seemed to carry the day, corruption and power, precious tools in the devil's tool box. There was a new storm joining the familiar one brewing off shore and careening toward the coastline of Haiti, sure to hit in hurricane fashion . . . the drug trade.

Aristide, former priest now politician, was elected president of Haiti in 1990, with international observers deeming the election largely free and fair. But with his radical populist policies and the violence carried out by his band of supporters, many of the country's elite became alarmed. His presidency was short lived and in September 1991, Aristide was overthrown in a coup d'état, during which hundreds were killed. Aristide was forced into exile and *General Raoul Cedras* and the military again seized power.

Under the brutal military rule of Cedras from 1991 until 1994, an estimated 3,000 to 5,000 Haitians were killed resulting in a large-scale exodus of refugees to the United States. The U.S. Coast Guard interdicted in excess of 41,000 Haitians during Cedras' period of brutal military rule, most of whom were denied entry into the U.S. and were repatriated back to Haiti. Boats over packed with Haitians often sank before reaching the U.S., the largest being the *Neptune* where 700 Haitians drowned in 1993, recorded as the worst ferry disaster in Haitian history.

The United Nations Security Council adopted *Resolution 940* in 1994, which authorized member states to use all necessary means to facilitate the departure of Haiti's military regime and restore Haiti's constitutionally elected government. U.S. troops prepared to intervene and were on the brink of an invasion in "Operation Uphold Democracy." President Clinton dispatched a negotiation team led by former President Jimmy Carter to convince the regime to step aside and allow for the reinstatement of constitutional rule. With U.S. troops on Haiti's doorstep, Cedras and other top leaders agreed to step down and Aristide returned to finish out his term. In the 1995 elections, Aristide's political coalition *Lavalas* (Waterfall), won a broad, sweeping victory. Renee Preval, a political ally of Aristide, was elected president. Preval's term ran from 1996 to 2001. The transition between Aristide and Preval was the first ever peaceful transition of power between two constitutionally elected presidents throughout all of Haiti's turbulent history.

It was in the middle of Preval's presidential term that I entered the chaotic scene and saga of Haiti's troubled history. Preval's presidency was fairly stable and relatively peaceful, but the heavy weight of profound poverty remained a heartbreak. There were still remnants of the US military in Haiti when I arrived in 1999, but its presence was minimal and was still there solely for infrastructure building and support purposes. It was not visible in public venues but was confined to an offsite, self contained compound away from the central city. It was reassuring to have them around however, no matter how remote they intended to be. The country just seemed to run better with U.S. military presence there, like having an adult in the room for stability and guidance, so it seemed in my observation of things. I arrived in the spring of that year. Within months, however, that security blanket was taken away and overnight it vanished, leaving me feeling a little naked. But that quickly wore off.

A rift had for some reason developed between Aristide and Preval, and the government once again began to descend into chaos, which is of course what Haiti seems to know best, so the unravelling of stability was not a surprise to anyone. In the November, 2002 elections, amid political squabbles and typical government dysfunction, Aristide was again elected president in an election that was boycotted by the opposition and in which only 50 percent of the voting public participated.[1]

---

1. The historical chronology described above is largely extracted from Wikipedia, "History of Haiti," some from my own experiential knowledge from living there, and Haitian folklore.

16

Expansion and Dysfunction

As we approached the Haitian coastline for the second time in a month for our permanent assignment, I marveled again at the natural beauty of the island set in the brilliance of the majestic blue waters from a distance, but I knew the reality on the streets below and that quickly brought me back into the reality of how life was really playing out on the ground.

When I reported for my new assignment in Port-au-Prince it coincided with a substantial expansion of the office in terms of agent personnel. Going from a minimal two-person Special Agent office, it instantly expanded to five, plus a supervisor Country Attaché. The strategic plan was for the DEA to take on a more enforcement-oriented role and to work closely with; to help train and mentor our Haitian narcotics police counterparts, within the newly formed Haitian National Police (HNP). The National Police had replaced the disbanded military. The task was kind of like trying to teach a toddler how to ride a bike, yet we tried nonetheless. But before long there began to emerge disturbing rumors of corruption within the national police ranks, and throughout the whole of government, for that matter, so we were faced with a tricky task and an up-hill battle to fight, or blindly ignore it. There seemed to be no real consensus or leadership on the matter so we took the narrow view of blindly trying to carry out our game plan, to swim upstream. Failure on the part of leadership to recognize the truth of what was really going on was frustrating, and even a little depressing for me during my first twelve months in Haiti. But I sat back and observed.

Our own haphazardly thrown together office also had its problems. It too had its own level of dysfunction, in part due to the eclectic array of personalities, lack of experience, and weak leadership. It could have had something to do with, "who wants to go to that rat hole Haiti anyway," mindset and the recruitment issues that such a perception posed. For my part, having recently gone through a divorce and not being particularly secure financially, I viewed the opportunity as one to inject some stability back into my financial affairs, which were a bit bleak at that moment in time. That reality, coupled with what had become for me a captivating intrigue to work in an overseas environment and the adventure it might offer, was an attractive package. I missed that intrigue and was energized to go seek and find it again. I did, but at some cost. That coupled with the constant rain and dreary weather in Seattle, very much in contrast to the tropical weather which I had grown accustomed to in Burma, was enough for me to look forward to new horizons, in sunny weather. Haiti offered the kind of inviting climate which I wholeheartedly welcomed. I also missed the cultural diversity. In theory, it was a hit.

The vast majority of DEA's several thousand Special Agent employees would very much prefer to work on the domestic front and remain among the familiar, as opposed to bending and melding into a different culture. But I felt drawn into the mosaic of God's creatures, different as they may express themselves throughout our amazing world, so off to Haiti I charged.

Who Designed this Puzzle?

The newly expanded and updated DEA office was an odd, hastily thrown together group in its composition. One might conceive on the surface that it made some sense with its mixture of female/male, black and white make up, but it was a poorly conceived mix of personalities and experience. There was the new Country Attaché who had no experience in a foreign country, or as a supervisor for that matter. He lacked experience and the strong character traits needed to take on the complexities of launching a new drug enforcement program in such a dysfunctional and unruly place such as Haiti. It was no fault of his, just a bad match.

There was Leduc, who was born in Haiti and put himself through college in the U.S., becoming a U.S. citizen, and then ultimately reaching his goal of being hired by the Drug Enforcement Administration. Obviously, Leduc understood very well the culture and personality of the Haitian people, but also knew the country's history and the futility of placing a lot of trust in the institution of the Haitian National Police. There was Sam, who had overseas experience with DEA in Nigeria, but didn't seem too interested in doing too much of anything except getting promoted. We had Todd, a

Kentucky boy with a law degree who had come from the Los Angeles Field Division, and while possessing a very bright intellect, spent an inordinate amount of energy on self-promotion and, I suspect, put in for the assignment to escape L.A. He could look forward, after a short two-year commitment, to benefit from the promise of getting a more desirable States side assignment at the end of it. And then there was Catherine, a very charming and cunning girl, also from L.A., who had dazzling looks and used them to her advantage, as well as to her detriment. I can't say that we bonded as a group, with each part in the organic scheme seeming to work in discord as opposed to desiring and striving to work in harmony and unity. I genuinely questioned how this experiment was going to work out. It didn't very well. There just wasn't purpose, vision, or direction that I could see; and it was hard for me to grasp where we were going with this mission.

Right from the start there was bad karma between the supervisor and me, and I struggled in trying to figure out the reason why. I generally always got along with people and it was my intention to do so in my new environment. Even in my early professional years while working at the State Prison, I got along with both the inmates and staff alike. One might consider that dealing with hardened criminals might be a challenge, but they were just people who for whatever reason made some serious mistakes. This supervisor of mine, in Haiti, not prison, left me perplexed. I considered that maybe I posed a threat to him in some way, possibly because I had overseas experience and he had none; or I felt comfortable and confident around various components of embassy personnel, and he did not; or possibly he sensed somehow, that I did not have confidence in him, that I thought he was not up to the task. That was certainly the case, but I worked very hard in trying not to convey that thought to him, but maybe, I possibly failed in that regard. I don't know.

Whatever the reason, I became aware early on that he was out to do me no good. This cast me into unchartered waters. Never in my life had I felt so much animosity from someone with authority over me, for no apparent reason. I had throughout my life always had an abundance of confidence in my natural ability to get along with diverse and different varieties of people. This was a difficult pill to swallow, let alone digest, and there were not many places to escape to when you're stuck on an island country, and confined to the limited relationships available in a relatively small embassy environment. I had never been a quitter and I was determined to tough it out, and with the help of strong, life giving, encouragement and backing from my wife, I did. I held out the secret hope, and hunch, that this guy would not survive the daunting challenges of Haiti's quirkiness and dysfunction for long. Embassy life is like living under a microscope. He would succumb to his own undoing, intuition informed me.

Trying to Make Sense of the Scene

It was a tough and trying time and a totally new experience for me. I resorted to unconventional ways to try to deal with the situation. I was reading a couple books on Buddhism that I had picked up somewhere, written by an American Zen Master. In his written words about the Buddha's practical wisdom, he offered some instruction on the spiritual art of finding peace by shedding the ego and self, which I strove very hard to do. It became a very intensive spiritual undertaking at the time. Did that help alleviate the pain I was experiencing? I don't know, maybe in the long view of life's never-ending challenges it did. A growth experience for sure though. Pain and suffering are germane to our humanity, and this I do know.

It got to be almost too much to take when the Assistant Special Agent in Charge (ASAC), came up from our Division Headquarters in San Juan, Puerto Rico to give us a "pep-talk." These meetings with him usually consisted of him going off the rails screaming at us about shaping up or shipping out, while mostly aiming his menacing stare at me. He probably saw a glazed-over stare back at him. I kept asking the question: "Why Lord?" I also kept wondering what my overly supportive boss was telling this guy about me. I was in a very difficult and painful place, in these unfamiliar, murky waters which I found myself swimming in.

Catholic theologian, Karl Rahner, S.J., suggests that God can be experienced in our dark times when life just seems to be working against us. During such times, we may experience the Divine Presence, as having a surprising ability to endure and to hope in the face of hardship and opposition. He points to this sustaining Source as the mysterious presence of the God of Light, upholding us in our "dark night." In some unfathomable way, we discover a Source of strength that goes beyond anything we can attribute to ourselves.

In his book, *The Enduring Heart, Spirituality for the Long Haul*, Wilkie Au cites Judith Viorst's best-selling book, *Necessary Losses*, where he refers to her notion of Christian spirituality that teaches, "we grow by losing and leaving and letting go." Au goes on to say that to journey successfully entails refusing to be derailed by the inevitable losses in life, and continuing to walk ahead with soul, trusting in the life-giving power of God available to us at every point on our journey. He maintains that Christian spirituality adds the fundamental belief that wherever we encounter diminishment and death in our lives, we can rely on the presence and power of God to be there to bring about new life in some mysterious way.[1] I had lost my self-esteem, in a way,

---

1. Au, *Enduring Heart*, 26–31.

and was going through an experience of dying to my fairly well-developed self-image. Even though I did not have access to these words of wisdom at the time, somehow, I knew I would pass over this crater in the tricky road I was navigating. I intuitively clung to that belief in the depths of my heart.

Unimaginative Approach to a Developing Problem Looming

The office strategic plan was to divide our group of agents into three teams with assignment locations at the nearby Port-au-Prince Seaport, a team at the main International Airport, and a team of two at large, to liaise with our Haitian counterparts. Todd and I drew the seaport duty where we had a makeshift office set up in a discarded trailer, formerly used as temporary office space at the Embassy while it was undergoing some physical restructuring and renovation. The off-site refuge was a blessing of sorts, because I had legitimate, existential reasons to want an escape from our DEA office at the Embassy, with all the suffocating bad karma in the air. It served well as a welcome escape from an intolerable environment.

Execution of the strategy, especially at the seaport, did not bear fruit from a drug enforcement stand point. Drug smuggling was not happening where Todd and I had been stationed, although in fairness to the developers of strategy, we didn't know that at the time. There did tend to be more activity for those assigned to the airport. If they had suspicions about cocaine being smuggled onto a flight bound for the U.S., they would notify DEA agents in Miami, New York or Boston. They could, and did, make seizures in those places, where drugs or other contraband would be dealt with appropriately and legally. Leaving loads of cocaine in the hands of the Haitian National Police to deal with was a bad idea, and not even a consideration amid the considerable corruption concerns.

On one occasion the Port-au-Prince airport detail failed to take notice of an innocuous, routine looking piece of luggage, leaving Port-au-Prince for LaGuardia Airport in New York. Authorities there did open the suitcase because anything coming from Haiti was always suspect, only to discover two decapitated human heads packed inside. I asked Haitian born and raised Leduc, what in the world was the meaning behind that disgusting discovery, and he bellowed in a matter-of-fact way, as if I should have known, "Voodoo!" "Oh," I said, somewhat shocked and even a bit shaken. Shocking to me, but not to my Haitian friend. That was reality in the culture of my present home, and place of sometimes unpleasant work, Haiti.

17

A Current of Sweet Grace and Relief from Grief

In welcome answer to my prayer, premonition and wish, the powers within the DEA complex in San Juan and Washington DC, did finally recognize the mistake they had made in their formulation of the office make-up, so hastily put together. With that realization, they wisely removed the one in charge of the dysfunctional disaster that was ours. Not only my antagonist was he, that was my problem to deal with, but for the greater benefit, clarity of vision and purpose of mission, the move was made. Nice thinking by somebody, I thought.

Gone from Haiti before his first year was completed, he was ultimately transferred to a domestic office in California where he wasn't overly challenged by having to manage a lot of people in an enforcement environment, especially in such an immensely challenging place as was Haiti, to his benefit and most probable relief. He was just in over his head. And for the release of that crushing weight suddenly being removed, I felt grateful and quiet joy. It was a good move all around. I'm sure he was feeling an overabundance of stress and pressure in that Haitian pressure cooker, and was secretly just happy to get out of there, and to get on with his life and career. So was I!

To this day I cannot fully comprehend why I was marked as a target for his passive aggressive tendential attitude toward me. Some behavior is just not explainable. I later ran into my old nemesis, turned amicable associate, in Los Angeles, while at a supervisor's conference of some kind, and he was surprisingly cordial. We had a conversation somewhat lacking in any real substance, but full to the brim with cordiality and friendly human exchange, in which language is not really a requisite. But there we were in conversation, verbal and nonverbal, friendly, and I was glad to have left that chapter in my life on a positive note and in harmony. Peace is a good thing. It is a door through which joy can be found.

Needless to say, life with the DEA got back to as normal as one could expect in a place such as Haiti. Sam was made the "Acting Country Attaché," until they could bring in someone at the appropriate pay grade and GS level. Hopefully that would be someone with some experience and a modicum of interpersonal skill. This would take nearly another year for the recruiting process and required language school to play out, however. We ditched the seaport component of our strategy, and returned to a more conventional way of going about our business. Sam was laid back and left me alone to do my job. He knew and respected that I had experience in both the domestic and foreign arenas of the DEA world. I went about the more conventional business of trying to recruit informants for intelligence purposes. The office chemistry was still not perfectly synchronized, but the atmosphere felt more peaceful and less dysfunctional. As a bonus, the Assistant Special Agent in Charge in Puerto Rico, who had paid occasional visits to Haiti to scream at us, maybe more so at me, retired. Life was looking better . . . much better.

Over the course of my second two-year tour in Haiti, with my comfort level vastly improved and with a much more developed sense of the place, I could set my sights on more creative ways of approaching the job. In the meantime, the country seemed to be falling back into its more usual, disconcerting character of dysfunction, with increasing corruption taking hold. Under Rene Preval's presidency, with the very recent memory of US Military presence still fresh in the collective mind of the country, there was an uncharacteristic sense of stability that seemed to prevail for a while. The U.S. had a nice, cooperative, relationship with him. But Aristide was re-elected President in 2001, after Preval's term had run its course, and the relationship became a bit more of a challenge.

Coinciding with Aristide's return to power was increasing evidence that drug traffickers, with the help of elements within the Haitian National Police, were becoming more brazen day by day. There were strategic spots throughout the country where stretches of road had been improved and built for the sole purpose of cocaine laden planes flying in from Colombia to land on. Certain bad actors within the HNP actually provided security for these off-load operations. There were still some upright, uncorrupted elements among the police ranks, but increasingly they became exceedingly more difficult to identify as time went on. Those who were in positions of power had to be very strong individuals to buck the tide of corruption seeping into the institution. It was shocking to witness the morphing phenomenon of degeneration occurring so rapidly. It just seemed a logical conclusion to make that the corruption had to be coming from the highest levels of government for it to be spreading so rapidly and blatantly throughout. I was developing a strong pet theory about the President himself.

Haiti was a choice transshipment location which trafficking organizations could salivate over. The table already set with its ripe geopolitical and socioeconomic environment; a poor country with poorly paid government officials susceptible to bribes; an inexperienced newly formed Haitian National Police, and a consistently unstable government. The country had the perfect cocktail of ingredients to make it a tasty and vulnerable morsel to devour, as well as an easy and accessible playground for drug traffickers with a voracious appetite to corrupt the weak with little resistance. The cartels would also recognize that the DEA, up to this point in time had given scant attention to Haiti, which made the playground atmosphere even more enticing. It was ripe for the picking. And like Eve in the garden, the temptation couldn't be resisted.

Unseemly, Irrevocable Evidence to Make the Case

One morning we were called by one of the few upstanding and trustworthy individuals, within the investigative branch of the HNP, with whom we worked closely. He informed us that a drug plane had crashed on a remote piece of road outside Port-au-Prince. Mario Andresol was the Chief in charge of all investigative branches of the HNP. We met him at the crash site, there to find a small Cessna aircraft off to the side of the narrow road, which had obviously crashed but was also substantially and intentionally torched. Then we saw the grizzly remains of two charred bodies, apparently the pilots, lying next to the burnt wreckage. Upon taking a careful look inside the damaged fuselage, we observed the plane's Colombian registration, a metal plate still preserved and intact. There were no obvious signs of the plane's cocaine cargo left behind, but there was no doubt in our minds, it had been there and subsequently removed by Haitian traffickers and their contingent of corrupt police, employed to ensure the security of the cargo and its safe off-load. Unable to fly the damaged plane from the site, it and the two pilots were unceremoniously destroyed by fire, along with any other potential pieces of evidence, so we concluded. That was an awakening for me as to the ruthlessness of these traffickers and their corrupt police facilitators with no soul. In that revulsive moment, a shock reverberated throughout my whole being as I stared into the devil's face on that barren road outside Port-au-Prince.

The scene depressed me, not only because of the violence and death inflicted on the Colombian pilots, but also because another reality struck with horrific implications in that moment. And I perceived it struck Mario the same way. Drug trafficking and smuggling cocaine loads into Haiti had become far too brazen and seemingly, almost sanctioned. It seemed to have become routine business. It was out in the open, although taking place in the dark of night, but with no apparent government interference. There seemed to be little attempt to hide it. I felt a pang of sadness and pity for Mario, a former military officer and a righteous person with integrity who took pride in his work and his position within the national police. It had to be a painful reality for him to try to reconcile. The system seemed to be turning against him and it was just a sad contradiction of justice to witness, in this person. I had a lot of pride in my own agency and in my work and I empathized with the disappointment he undoubtedly was feeling about his country and the lack of integrity becoming so much the norm, stoic as he was. Another reality also came into focus for me in that moment; government complicity had to be sanctioned from a place far above his own rather vaunted position. At least this was the thread of dominant reasoning being sewn into my world of logic. The suspicion would later become conviction, as events would play out and reveal truth. The way I would approach and conduct my work in Haiti would now be one evolving into a dramatically different strategic plan as this new reality became, sadly but undeniably, clearer. My vision was changing and began to do so in radical fashion that sunny, charred morning.

Not long after that event, Mario was forced to leave Haiti and take refuge in the United States, because his life was now existentially in danger. He was too close to the heart beat of the corrupt monster and was too much a threat to its life line. He apparently had more than just a clue as to who within the government was complicit in the burnt plane affair, the murder of the two pilots, and the provision of protection for the ever-increasing number of loads of cocaine being brought into the country. If so, he became a threat to an evil more powerful than he himself could withstand and remain alive, but he also would not betray his principles and become subservient to that evil.

Mario had impressive virtues of fortitude and purpose that fed his conscience and actions, but he also had an obligation to preserve his life. The combination of feelings welling up in that moment earlier at the crash site, Mario dejectedly standing at the site of the destruction, along with his subsequent submission to surrender and ultimate distress-call for asylum, saddened me in no small way. Standing there with him, cemented my conviction and resolve to change course and root out the evil core, where ever it buried its head in the labyrinth of corruption in this land, no matter how deep or high up the ladder it went. It was a sober and serious moment in the history of Haiti, set within the recurring familiar story of deterioration and corruption. A new sketch of the same old scenery in Haitian affairs was being drawn. The cycle of corruption again remerging, was now a recognizable reality once again. Mario would be missed.

Guard de Cote, a Respite and Retreat

The relatively newly instituted Haitian National Police had numerous bureaus and departments like any large metropolitan police department in the U.S. The Haitian Coast Guard (Guard de Cote) fell under the HNP umbrella and amazingly did not seem to fall victim to the spreading disease of corruption which was metastasizing throughout the rest of Haitian officialdom. There were a couple plausible theories for this phenomenon, I reasoned. The first was that its commander, Leon Charles, also a former officer in the disbanded Haitian military, was another stand up person with strong character and virtue. The Guard de Cote headquarters was physically set apart and somewhat remote from the rest of other government entities that fell under the spell of corrupt influences. They more or less existed in their own cloistered world under Charles' steady and focused command.

The Guard de Cote was set off from the city's crumbled and dirty center, a couple miles down the coast on the Port-au-Prince Bay. Their location was actually a rather serene spot with greenery on land and of course the water access opening up to the beautiful blue waters of the Caribbean Sea inlet. During my early tumultuous period in Haiti, I loved to visit with Leon and others under his command in that comparatively serene setting. Occasionally, we would take excursions out into the waters on one of the faster patrol boats, into some of the more beautiful and peaceful areas of the country, away from land. These mini retreats were welcomed and served the purpose of re-establishing a sense of peacefulness and equilibrium, with the blending of air and sea momentarily and magically softening the salty sting of discord. Out on the water we could take in the serene images of solitary fishermen in their handcrafted boats, striving for their livelihood on the quiet waters. The only unsettling observance though, was all the garbage and plastic trash that could be seen floating in the otherwise pristine waters. That was sad to see, a beautiful planet abused by ignorance.

Guard d' Cote did not offer any imaginable advantage or disadvantage to the drug cartels, already smuggling large shipments of cocaine to the United States through Haiti. They had nothing to offer the cartels, nor were they a threat to them by way of significant interference.

Already having other institutionalized means of trafficking systems in place, and having no fear of any enforcement threat from the Guard d' Cote, they were left alone to be who they were, largely untouched by corruption, or tempted to become so.

Mark, the Coast Guard and a Ship from Denmark

I first met Captain Mark Cawthorn, new arrival at the Embassy, while standing on the front steps of the entrance to the place one morning. I was immediately, instinctively drawn to him and had a wild hunch that I would like to get to know him. Maybe I sensed the "wild" in him that I was always drawn to, in people or things. He had a confident air about him, was approachable, and was witty in a dry sort of way. We quickly hit it off and soon struck up a friendship. He had a rather sarcastic, irreverent sense of humor, but he was also a kind and caring person. He took his job very seriously but had fun with it also. His primary function, that of mentoring the Guard de Cote, he performed with focused attention and purpose. All in all, Mark was a colorful and sharp addition to the Embassy's Country Team. Personal relationships among my DEA coworkers still not what I would regard as warm, Mark's arrival at the Embassy came at the right time to improve the overall work environment for me. While I got along with the other Coast Guard Liaison Officers that preceded him, Mark was different. I needed a friend at that time with whom I could laugh and just enjoy being around. No competition, no comparing, just a person with whom I could just hang out and feel comfortable being around. I considered his arrival a gift from above at that particular trying time. I do think God is always watching out for our needs, even when we are not always attentive to that special, caring gift that is available to us all.

"Official Intelligence" information was brought to our attention one day, I don't recall through what channel specifically, but most likely it was from the National Security Agency (NSA). A Panamanian flagged vessel would be arriving from Colombia with a legitimate cargo of sugar, and buried within the ship's bowels, an illegitimate cargo of cocaine, so we were told. We; DEA, Haitian Coast Guard, and Mark eagerly jumped on this bit of enticing news with some excitement, tempered with a bit of skepticism, as the ship finally arrived in port, being escorted by Haitian tug boats.

The ship's Captain was from Denmark, and upon meeting and interviewing him, I was left with a favorable impression. He presented a very professional persona, was respectful and very cooperative. We spent over a week with him as the ship's cargo of sugar was off-loaded, all the while on the lookout for anything at all suspicious. The ship's commercial cargo consisted of thousands upon thousands of 50-pound bags of sugar, each of which was individually carried off from the sweltering cargo hold in the ship's belly. The bare-chested longshore workers with chiseled bodies were fortunate to have steady employment at the seaport, but I was amazed at the hard labor they carried out, eight hours a day, nonstop. To maintain their energy level, they would occasionally pick up a handful of sugar taken from a broken bag and shovel it into their mouths. There was not an ounce of fat on any of them, however. They worked in stone silence to conserve energy.

When the ship was finally emptied, Mark, with his expertise and training in search techniques and I, not so trained in that arena, scoured the empty vessel, conducting a thorough inspection of every nook and cranny where 500 kilograms of cocaine could conceivably have been stashed. We even had a US Customs drug dog flown in from Puerto Rico to take a crack at sniffing out any evidence of contraband. Nothing! These dogs don't miss, unless they're drunk. The ship was clean and the captain was vindicated, which actually was to our delight because we had gotten to know him pretty well and had grown to like and respect him. A true professional who didn't need more trouble than what he had already encountered.

During the nearly two weeks for the off-load process to unfold we had gotten to know the captain and his story quite well. He was an affable and smart professional who during the duration of his disruptive Haitian experience provided us some intriguing tutorial on Denmark's culture, and educated us on its history and royal past, as well as Viking and Valhalla lore. He even treated us to some of his rum reserves when the work day was finished, and the hard-working Haitian longshore men slowly dragged themselves from the docks and their weary bodies home.

For some perplexing reason, the Haitian port authorities would not clear the ship to leave port after we had declared it a drug free zone. It began to appear to me, the captain, and Mark, as though someone in the government was just trying to shake the shipping line down for cash. Maybe this sort of trickery and chicanery is not so uncommon in poor, third world countries around the globe, but it felt, and looked suspicious and maybe even a bit criminal to us. It was also a bit embarrassing to Mark and me since we had launched the fiasco in the first place.

Beginning to feel a little sorry for the captain, under the frustrating circumstances and appearance of corrupt shenanigans, we decided to invite the Captain from Denmark to my residence one evening, where my wife had prepared a wonderful dinner to ameliorate the sticky situation. We had a great party, with food, swimming in our pool, and the captain's rum, to lighten up the burdensome quandary a bit for him. A couple days later Mark decided to take the distorted situation into his own hands. On a bright, sunny morning, as most are in Haiti, Mark and I went down to the sea port; and with no regard for the Haitian Port Authority, Mark told the captain to set sail, which he did; Mark and I standing at the end of the pier happily watching the empty ship sail off into the Caribbean Sea. No one dared challenge us. The only ones who could have done anything about the ship's escape into the open sea would have been the Haitian Coast Guard and they were not about to try. It was a satisfying moment, like freeing a hostage after being held in captivity, unjustly, for too long. Standing at the end of that pier, feeling the freedom that was now the captain's and his crew, was a rare moment of exhilaration for me in Haiti, up to that point. It left me smiling for the rest of the day and beyond.

Hypolite and a Somber, Shocking Shift in Sensibility

Le Bureau de Lutte Contre le Traffic de Stupefiants (BLTS) was the HNP's narcotics bureau and fell under the broader Criminal Investigation Division of the HNP, which had been under Mario Andresol's command before he was forced to run for his life. I don't know what specific threats he had received but they had to have been serious ones.

The supervisor of the BLTS was another trusted individual DEA looked to as reliable and also as an ally. Hypolite Edmonds whom we had a good relationship with, was a likeable, intelligent, and dependable guy, who Commander Leon Charles of the Haitian Coast Guard thought highly of. Charles gave him his total and confident endorsement for being trustworthy, which were welcome words to hear in the swelling sea of corruption becoming more manifest within the HNP and government at large. We had countless meetings with Hypolite discussing theoretical approaches to narcotics enforcement strategies amid growing corruption concerns. He seemed not to be overly anxious to delve into the murky mixture of contradictions that were the reality in his world, and understandably so. We held onto guarded hope, however, that a relationship of integrity between the DEA and the BLTS could become the standard, of sorts, with Hypolite's strong character and values at the helm. That was before Mario received death threats that forced him to flee the country. Now the picture was rapidly changing and going downhill, like mud slides off the mountains during the rainy season.

We had put on training classes for the BLTS and Guard de Cote, and even went so far on one occasion to bring certain members of the Guard de Cote and BLTS to Miami for training and orientation with the US Coast Guard and US Customs. On the first morning of our program, we walked into the Miami Customs Regional Headquarters office where there were television sets on, and noticed that the eyes of employees all around were intently locked onto them. The TVs were showing the unthinkable, graphic, and horrifying scenes of the first of New York's Twin towers aflame, with half of a 747 stuck directly into the outer wall of the South building, the front half of the plane buried inside. There were huge plumes of smoke billowing out from the upper portion of the once magnificent tower tickling the sky. "What happened?" The question was on the stunned minds of everyone whose eyes were staring in shocked disbelief at the TV monitors. What kind of accident could this be, I thought, observing an unthinkable catastrophic, unexplainable event? Then its twin building was hit by a second 747 jumbo jet, this one caught in real-time on TV to the horror of every one watching. It immediately became shockingly clear that the United States of America was under attack. It was the sickest feeling I had ever felt in my entire life. Our training was understandably, abruptly cancelled and I went back to our hotel and spent the rest of the day stunned and saddened, watching the news with my wife, unable to speak.

The following morning, we turned our attention to the complex problem of getting everyone back to Haiti, as there were going to be very limited flights, if any, out of Miami. Over the course of days, we eventually managed to get all the Haitian people back home to Haiti as more commercial flights slowly began to be released back into the skies. The world, our world had changed and would never look the same.

Another Star Fallen from the Haitian Sky

Back in Haiti, life and the Haitian struggle went on with little having changed. It was impossible however, to not have thoughts compulsively jerked violently back to the unthinkable, tragic scene in New York City with heavy hearts grieving for the lives lost and those affected by the unthinkable event. A thought shared by, most likely, every American with a heart and soul.

Corruption continued its onward march toward a more pervasive reality within the Haitian National Police, and seemed as though it was becoming the norm rather than the exception. One early morning we were frantically contacted by a distraught Hypolite, who reported that during the night his home had been under siege and was violently shot up. He was particularly fearful for the safety of his young wife and baby girl who could have been readily killed during the vicious onslaught. This intimidation tactic was obviously a clear signal by unidentified assailants that Hypolite needed to be extremely concerned for the safety of his own life and that of his family. These villainous cowards had no tolerance for any upstanding narcotics agent in their midst. The violent attack on Hypolite's home was most likely not carried out by drug traffickers, who would naturally be inclined to want to avoid attracting attention to themselves or their activities, but more probably by corrupt, criminal, components of the police who did not want anyone around who had any iota of recourse to, or affiliation with the DEA to interfere with the lucrative narcotics trade and their own handsome profits from it.

Hypolite and his wife had US visas and could escape the danger by leaving the country quickly, and they did, rightly so. Their baby girl did not have a visa for entry into the U.S. and needed a few days to obtain one, as well as a passport. She was left in the care of her Aunt while friends at the American Embassy arranged for her travel documents. Once the proper documents were expeditiously processed, Todd, from our office and his wife, escorted the infant to Boston to be reunited with her anxious and extremely grateful parents, to the relief of the young family and everyone involved with them.

They were safely reunited, but the sickening and sad picture that was being portrayed now, with the dramatic life-threatening scenarios and hasty exits of Mario and Hypolite from Haiti, was serious and quite telling of the contemporary landscape taking form in the country. Haiti had quickly transformed its face to a much darker shade of dark again, almost overnight. I now completely changed the lens through which I viewed Haiti and its National Police, and with it a much clearer vision with which to understand the task at hand. The new vision, like after a cataract surgery, offered enhanced vision with greater imagination and meaning. Don't change things that can't be changed; attack them and destroy the root evil, which will ultimately effect change, became my mantra. It was the last I ever saw of Hypolite, with whom I had grown fond of. And I wish him well.

It also became startlingly apparent to me that we could no longer have a meaningful working relationship with the BLTS after what had transpired with Mario and Hypolite. That reality was perfectly clear. Either sinister powers from within the ranks of the National Police were subverting anti-narcotics efforts on behalf of the BLTS, or corruption had taken hold within its own ranks. I later came to realize that it was both. This brush fire was out of control. There were rumors afloat that Hypolite's replacement, Events Bryant, was working in collusion with the drug traffickers. DEA polygraphers came from Miami to administer "lie detector" tests to Bryant, already suspect of being corrupt, and all other members of the BLTS. Bryant surprisingly passed it, but the chief examiner of the program explained to me that polygraphs are not fool proof. "They can be beat," he simply stated. It later became evident that his statement was clearly true, Bryant was indeed thoroughly corrupt and later proven guilty, as I had suspected.

18

Could have Been Fiction
... But it Wasn't

In the meantime, amid these events, we had received word that the infamous, by way of innuendo, HNP Commander from the Northern Division Headquarters in Cap Haitian, Guy Philippe, wanted a meeting. He was a notorious figure, vaguely known to the DEA. Stories about Guy (pronounced Gee) were swirling around that he was protecting plane loads of cocaine being flown into his area of responsibility in the North, from Colombia. It was somewhat vague folklore, however. I didn't know what to believe any more. I was a little skeptical about these reports because others also vouched for his integrity and veracity. Guy was also a former officer in Haiti's defunct military. The stories about him were unverified, but so the tales went. I saw this as a potential opportunity to mix things up and jumped at the chance to meet with him. Unfortunately, I had the wrong person as a partner with me when we met Guy. We had different philosophical approaches as to what the overarching strategy with Guy would be, but it was still an intriguing prospective opportunity for something to come of it. I had worked on more than a few conspiracy cases in my career and my thoughts ran along those lines. My partner was relatively new to DEA, and his experience was limited to working at the Los Angeles International Airport (LAX), so our visions would be different based on our experience and tendencies. I now had my sights set on the President and thought Guy might be a possible vehicle to get there.

Our initial encounter with Guy was at the Petionville Club, which was a private facility that included a restaurant, a large swimming pool, gym, tennis courts and a field on the side of a small mountain which they referred to as the "Petionville Golf Course." It was the only such designated piece of real estate in Haiti, so we made due when it came to "playing golf." As golf courses go it was depressing, like much of Haiti, so we just had to use our imaginative vision. But in spite of the need for imagination, I found myself there every weekend pretending it was a real golf course. I was usually accompanied by other colleagues from the Embassy or foreigners from elsewhere who were members of the club and who loved the game so much they played despite having to dodge a goat or chickens walking on what was supposed to serve as a putting green. Imagination!

On this particular Sunday I arrived at the Club before "tee time" to meet with Guy. Despite his very robust reputation as a person of influence and sway, I was surprised to see he was a rather demur individual in stature, but not at all lacking in copious amounts of energy and charisma. Toting a reputation as being a cohort among major drug traffickers, I found him to be intriguing and likeable. His high energy and big smile made me even more skeptical about the rumors swirling about him. Guy introduced his simple looking wife from Wisconsin, which struck me as an odd arrangement. This to me looked to be a very different picture than what expectations would have painted. She was a friendly, seemingly simplistic, midwestern girl. Odd image to inject into his storied persona.

We spent a half hour or so getting acquainted, as Guy clearly expressed his razor-like focus on his dislike for, and unabashed intent to get Aristide removed from office. His president was unfit and corrupt, he adamantly proclaimed. Guy enthusiastically espoused the idea of a possible coup d'état in his rather lighthearted, boyish way. He quite simply, yet with an eye-popping amount of naiveté, audaciously, yet sincerely, expressed his desire for the DEA and the American Embassy to help with logistics and weapons to depose the mad man! That took my mind off golf momentarily, and got my heart racing after his own heart. His intention, not his method, sent my mind flying into the stratosphere.

I explained to Guy that we could potentially make a criminal case against Aristide, with his cooperation. My partner wanted nothing to do with where this conversation was heading, and our initial meeting stalled out fairly quickly. My initial reaction to what Guy was saying was one of mild shock. DEA was not in the business of coups and starting civil wars. Although I detected some naiveté in Guy's fantasy, he apparently was sincere. I also accepted the encounter with him to be a potential coup of my own if I could secure his cooperation. There was, in my view, real potential for my own fantasy and refocused mission to make a case against Aristide. Not violently though. But in my imagination, in a more legalistic and legitimate way, our collaboration had huge potential to bear fruit. Excitement grew in me as I set my mind to nurture this new relationship.

Guy was the product of Haiti's violent history of overthrowing its leaders, so I guess I could understand where he was coming from, in some way. In light of that I shouldn't have been shocked by his proposal. Guy and I had a similar goal but our means to the end seemed to differ quite a bit. But there was room to come to an understanding, I thought. It had been a very general somewhat vague conversation, but I had hopes there might be real potential for something to develop with him, in a more legitimate and conventional way. I left our meeting with a feeling of affinity for Guy after that first encounter, crazy as I thought his plan was. Was the feeling of affinity for him because of him, or our shared interests? I'm not sure. I did share his perspective though; this president was no good, and a criminal.

I had a follow up meeting with Guy several days later which again was mostly about getting to know each other and continuing to debate which approach to our mutual goal was the wisest course of action. I certainly could not conspire with him in planning a coup. I felt though, that we had formed a bond of sorts, through our mutual interest, and I intended to pursue our relationship. Guy, in his charismatic dimension of expression, spoke about his desire to oust Aristide violently, and of his disdain for the President's corrupt government. While airing his fantasy of a coup d'état, he was a little coy about specifics, avoiding a complete indictment of himself. I was confident in my ability to ultimately persuade him to work with me to make a legal case against Aristide. But I kept having to shift the conversation away from a violent takeover, to what he could tell me about the President's corrupt activities in order to build a case for conspiracy. These two meetings with Guy were still preliminary in nature, though.

We met with Guy a third time at my house, in the evening. This encounter, however, took on a much more serious nature, and with more vivid detail about his intentions for planning a coup. He wanted the "United States Government through the DEA" to provide him with guns and logistics support to carry out his bold, cockamamy plan. The U.S has always been about the business of building and supporting democracy in Haiti, not supporting its history of violent take overs of power.

Guy sounded convincing in that he had the support from enough backers in the country to be successful with his plan, but just needed the armament and U.S. backing to pull it off. This sounded like story book stuff, but given Haiti's history, I guess maybe it wasn't. I had no intention of seriously entertaining such an endorsement and told him evenly that it was an illegal proposition and the U.S. Government would never consider such an approach because it would essentially be an act of war on a legally elected

President. I tried to convince him that my approach of a criminal indictment was the legal, sensible, and morale one, and much less messy. We just don't do coups as a matter of international diplomacy . . . usually.

I did not convince him, but I knew he could not pull his plan off without help in procuring sufficient arms from our government. Because he didn't have the means, I did not consider that Haiti's current government was facing a credible threat from Guy Phillipe at this stage. I was intrigued by his brazen boldness and passion. It collided with his charm and boyish naiveite, painting an almost unrecognizable picture to reconcile. A former military officer in recent history, the United States forced Haiti to dissolve the military and replace it with the national police force. Phillipe's brazen intentions of a forcible ousting of Aristide did not shock me in that context, but imagining the U.S. would back it up, did.

I thought it was a little premature to pull the trigger on Guy just yet because he did not have the capability at this juncture to be an existential threat to the government at this moment in time. He did confirm for me what I had been thinking though, Aristide was indeed a bad actor who Guy sincerely believed had to go and was willing to risk his life to make it happen. I respected his resolve and proactive courageous intention, but his ultra-alfa persona caused him to be a bit misguided in his own judgment and decision-making processes.

There was no pretension or false bravado in Guy's proposal. He was sincere and I respected his passion for the country and ultimate purpose, even if he was possibly motivated to some degree by his own desire for power. I don't know. From my perspective it made him likeable and the sort of person I was naturally attracted to, reckless and daring . . . passionate. He was full of purpose, dreaming the big dream, misplaced as it maybe was. We agreed to talk further, however, we would not get that chance.

The following day at the Embassy, my "partner," without any input from me, took it upon himself to go directly to the Deputy Chief of Mission and inform him that Guy Phillipe was planning a coup d'état to overthrow Aristide. I thought Todd was a bit too anxious to win favor with those in power at the Embassy, seeking to look like the privileged informed hero of the tall tale. To me it appeared he could not restrain himself from the temptation of being the herald of such juicy news, dripping with drama and intrigue. I was not at all convinced his intentions were motivated solely by moral convictions of good conscience, over self-serving ones. I won't be the judge of that, but I was sadly disappointed and felt slightly betrayed.

Adhering to proper protocol, however, the DCM, a respectable man who knew his way around State Department obligations and intricacies, reasoned that he was obliged by law to inform the Government of Haiti of this development, without factoring in that Guy did not have the means at his disposal to carry out such an audacious project. I thought at the time, it was a bit of an overreaction as well as a huge missed opportunity to work Guy into a more reasonable, cooperative, and effective scheme to solve the problem of Aristide. I did not have a legal argument to make, in my assessment of the situation; but thought in the moment, there was an opportunity missed, and now a life in imminent danger. I discreetly gave Guy a call and told him I needed to see him when I got home from work. It was an emergency!

When I got back to my residence around 6:pm, I contacted Guy and told him to meet me there. As I stood on my balcony half way up the Rue Paco Mountain, I saw a train of black SUV's careening toward my place, blue emergency lights flashing. Guy had a small army of security cops with him and seemed to already sense the gravity of the situation. The group of police serving as his security detail were some of the biggest Haitians I had ever seen. Guy, being rather small himself was dwarfed among them. He and they walked through my house and out onto the patio where I was waiting, serenely observing the panoramic view of the city below. From the height and distance of the balcony, the sad city of Port-au-Prince actually looked pretty at night, when all one could see were the sprinkling and sparkle of city lights in the distance.

Guy sat down for a moment. Without pleasantries, I directly told him that word of his plan had been exposed and I could do nothing about it. I did have a moral obligation to protect him from serious harm or even death, so I reasoned, although I didn't need a reason; it was instinct that took over. I had grown to like Guy and I very much felt his life was in danger. I needed to act to save that life.

Guy did not sit for long. More serious than I had ever seen him, he simply said thank you, rose from his chair, and abruptly departed. I never saw Guy again, but was informed that he had fled the country successfully and was safe in Nicaragua. About two weeks later my cell phone went off while I was in the Embassy cafeteria having lunch. I walked outside as I answered the call, and the now familiar voice on the other end simply said: "David, thank you. You saved my life." I told him to take care and the call ended.

I do not doubt that my conversation with Guy during that phone call was intercepted by our own embassy spy apparatus, because I know how that stuff goes at U.S. embassies in foreign countries. But I never heard a peep from anyone about it. After all, I did save his life and in the Haitian composition of collective history, that was a good thing. Guy would be back.

19

Open the Windows and Let the Fresh Air In

Things changed dramatically for the better almost overnight in the Port-au-Prince Country Office. Gone were Greg, Sam, Cathy, Rudy, and Todd. In came Al as the Country Attaché, Alex, Ernie, and Herman. The climate went from a suffocating, restrictive, rather self-centered environment to a refreshing, open, and cheerful one. Obas remained, but that was a positive thing. He brought with him to the office his own unique character and charm, and interacted well with the others. It felt like Springtime after a cold dark winter, with blooming flowers, sunshine and warmth. The windows were opened wide and welcoming fresh air rushed in. My world had dramatically changed almost instantly, turning from darkness to light, a fresh new dawn where there was laughter and good cheer. There was a warmth in the office stoked by positive attitudes toward one another that weren't self-serving and inward looking. Good things happen for those who wait and hope.

Obas knew Al from their time working together in Miami which helped the group's integration. Al was not alien to Haitian issues because of his experience in Miami. He also had connections and friends in the Caribbean Islands and a general feel for the region and its culture. Al was laid back, a very decent human being, and friendly. Over all, there suddenly had been lifted the heaviness, replaced by a feeling of lightness in the office and a general sense of energy turning toward a positive disposition. I had signed up for a second two-year tour and immediately knew I had made the right choice. A new direction for our mission took form right away, and the familiar, creative approach to DEA's more typical model of being proactive was back in our vernacular. This was my comfort zone and preferred perspective through which to interpret and act out our reality, given the particular environment.

Obas, who I affectionately referred to as "Obee," wanted nothing to do with administrative matters or directing others, so Al made me his back-up and the Acting Country Attaché in his absence. It was a completely new environment, for the better, and I had a new lease on life and my job. Both the picture and script had changed. There were also new folks in the hierarchy over in Puerto Rico, to whom we, and all other Caribbean DEA offices reported to. Al had an amicable relationship with the Special Agent in Charge there going back years. Because Al thought well of me, so did the new bosses in San Juan. Life was good again. All I could say was: "What a turnaround!" It made my head spin, but it felt so good I wanted to dance.

Identifying Allies

I set out on a course independent of the BLTS and the rest of the now rot infested HNP. There were more and more rumblings that the protection of drug traffickers and their illicit trade, went all the way to the top, generating handsome profits reaped from the unholy marriage. My interpretation of the "top" was the Office of the President. I had resolved, long before now I would find a way to take Aristide down, if that indeed was the case; and it was starting to appear more likely than not that it was the case.

I had come to conclude that it was useless to even think we could do anything meaningful in the fight against drug trafficking with our Haitian counterparts, the BLTS. Since Hypolite had been run out of the country they had become corrupt also, which was fast becoming a trendy model of operation for the police in Haiti. With the Agency's new Chief believed to be in the pocket of the traffickers, the former way of thinking was out of date and irrelevant now.

In the office we had some discussions about forming a team, of sorts, of those within the HNP who could be trusted to carry out special projects; such as capturing and bringing to the U.S. notorious figures such as Jacques Ketant for prosecution, or soon to be indicted Kingpin, Jean Eliobert Jasme. These were monumental mountains to climb in the corruption infested environment of Haiti where the President himself seemed to be on top of the decaying heap.

There was an individual whom Obas vouched for within a rather unique unit of the HNP, that he said could be trusted and was of good character. But I wondered how a person could maintain good character in an environment exerting such a strong, contrary current of evil tugging in the opposite direction. That may be possible for persons who have somehow developed very strong character. It could be, I came to realize. There were a few of those. A tricky and difficult world to navigate to be sure. Maybe even a little depressing, but quite possible to hold onto a sense of equilibrium with good values, with the aid of a little grace and a strong will.

I'll refer to Obas' referral as Francois. We approached him about our idea to form a small but trustworthy team. He declined our invitation, stating reasonable objections: his well-being, fear for his life, and it also would most likely not be good for his career; all of which was totally understandable, in the context of Mario and Hypolite's fate. François did, however, have a brother who he did not disclose during our recruitment encounter but would later emerge as an integral component and critical piece in the plot yet to be conceived.

One enigmatic character on "our side," in the complicated Haitian tapestry, who had some influence around town, was Renaud. A native Haitian, Renaud seemed to be somewhat connected with some of the influential elements of Haitian society and their role in it, in a somewhat mysterious way. He held a position, in some official capacity, at the Port-au-Prince International Airport, unclear as it was. He also had some kind of undefined relationship with certain people at the U.S. Embassy. He was a unique, somewhat mysterious individual planted in the Haitian scenery, whose exact function in the overall landscape was a bit opaque. He also seemed to have some undefined status within the U.S. Embassy, and could occasionally be encountered at diplomatic functions.

Renaud did "work" for us, in so far as he was usually accurate in providing intelligence relative to movements within the Haitian government, and identifying key Haitian officials and their activity as it related to the drug trafficking world. In other words, he was a "cooperating individual." In Renaud's seemingly official capacity at the Airport, he facilitated our travel when flying out of, or back into Haiti. He was a bit of an enigma but helpful, especially at the airport, and was seemingly trustworthy.

Given all these oblique variables placed into one colorful basket of uncolored eggs, I somewhat suspected he had a close connection to the CIA, based upon many factors; his living accommodations and obvious middle-class status, without any visible means of making a living to support that status. Most Haitians with comparable life styles and living accommodations were either successful business people, drug traffickers, or corrupt government officials. I ruled out all three options for him. In my mind it would not be out of character for the CIA to plant him in our world so as to keep tabs on what we as DEA were up to. That seemed logical given the dynamics of the drug trafficking enterprise in Haiti, currently woven into the fabric of official Haitian politics, and the influence it came to claim on the country. DEA was central in the mix of this potent dynamic. So, for the CIA to install one of their own in our midst made sense. It became my favorite theory about Renaud. It drove him crazy though, because he wanted information from me, and not, more appropriately, the other way around.

When I began to sense this relationship reversal, I just became coyer around Renaud. When he suspected I had major things developing in my own DEA world of intrigue, he began to press me about what I was up to. That only gave more credence to my theory about him and added jocularity to our interactions, from my perspective anyway. No problem. It now became a game for me to play with the CIA. He was possibly failing to deliver on the expectations of his true bosses. I didn't need another government agency muddling up my strategic plan though, sensitive and complicated as it was. I was already facing the challenge and complex duality of the Haitian government, the drug traffickers, and their allegiance to the devil. A complicated mixture of balls to juggle and not drop. I eventually zipped my lips around Renaud, but continued on with him in professional cordiality, and respect. It was a balancing act, as was everything else going on in this exceedingly complicated, but exhilarating new world of the Haitian Sensation.

Sam, my Man

Renaud was aware of our need to find a few good men to help out with the lofty goals I had in mind, but locating those kinds of individuals was a challenge, and getting them to cooperate was even a bigger one. Not long after our stab at the recruitment of Francois, I was approached by Renaud who told me he wanted me to meet someone who wanted to help out with the cause. I said "sure!" Renaud brought Sam to the Embassy where we were introduced. Sam spoke English pretty well, and seemed to be very Americanized. He was young but worldly at the same time. I liked him immediately and set up future meetings with him in order to get more acquainted and get a feel for how a working relationship might look like. This was Francois' brother, as it turned out. It was a serendipity moment.

Sam Moreau, a native Haitian, had recently relocated to Haiti from Florida where he had been living and studying in Miami. He recently had been invited by the President to return to Haiti to work at the Presidential Palace in an official capacity. Sam was brought back to work as a "special projects" person, having expertise in computer programming and technology.

He was additionally given some kind of special status as an "official" with some sort of non-descript law enforcement authority, which left me wondering what his role really was. An odd compilation of credentials, but I was open and intrigued to hear more about his resume and peculiar, special status within the Presidential Palace's power structure. The bottom line was, I intuitively liked him. There was no pretense, or hint of self-promotion whatsoever in him. He just impressed me as being the real deal who wanted to do the right thing. That was a waft of fresh cool air to breath in the moment.

Sam was fresh, he was clean and he was bold. He was what I needed for the dirty work that lie ahead. I grew to really like and respect him as we became more familiar with each other. His enthusiasm was infectious and his position at the Presidential Palace was perfect positioning. Did it occur to me that he might also have CIA connections? Yes, possibly, because Renaud brought him to me, but that didn't really matter. Sam would be an asset and would eventually prove himself to be a friend. He wanted to help and he was not afraid to jump into the deep, turbulent, nasty waters of Haiti's corruption with both feet. That was my gut instinct and I let it guide me without a moment's hesitation. Instinct can sometimes be the brightest light in revealing truth

Sam held a green card in the U.S. and was practically American in style and demeanor, but born and raised in Haiti, he knew his way around both systems and cultures. An employee of the Palace, Sam had privileged credentials, in addition to his own unique abilities to stay above and navigate through the morass of corruption, intimidation and powers of influence insidiously infiltrating many institutions of government. It was an odd situation because Sam obviously had a relationship with the President, who he knew I thought was corrupt, and knew also that I wanted to capture Jacques Ketant who had a special relationship with the President. It was a tangle of logical thinking to unravel but as it turned out none of that mattered to Sam. His loyalty was with the U.S. Government and law enforcement, more specifically the DEA; because of the drug trafficking invasion and existential epidemic invading and destroying his homeland. He wanted to do what was in the best interests of Haiti. I could read that in his demeanor, words, and spirit. I sensed that truth quite clearly in Sam. He was my man.

I thought about this paradox more than a little; the President picking bad fruit from drug trafficking, the recruitment of Sam into his unholy den of power, and Sam's seemingly blind quest to undo the underworld of the president's agenda. But as time went on, I grew more confident that Sam wanted to do the right thing and was committed to doing so. One of those few, rare individuals operating in the space of grace. "There are a few." As I got to know him, I began to feel that he was truly one of the good guys of the world. That struck a chord, especially after telling me one day of his intention to send his wife and daughter back to Miami due to the danger working with us could pose to his family. That sacrificial, precautionary move spoke volumes about his dedication and commitment to get things right in his country. He was serious about it. Working with the DEA to that end, in the current environment, was probably the straightest path to accomplishing his goal, but also a very dangerous proposition. I had a strong "sense" we were meant for each other in that moment of time, and felt a surge of confidence that we would get the job done. Sam gave a shot of adrenaline to me; synergy at work in unseen ways.

20

Earning the Title "Kingpin" Requires Being Best in the Trade

Certain high-level heads of trafficking organizations throughout the world earned the right to be labelled "Drug Kingpins," and were so designated after consideration and consensus by a consortium consisting of the DEA, CIA, and the State Department as well as any other relevant Embassy, National Security component. One such Haitian designee deserving of the title was Jean Eliobert Jasme, who was simply known as "Eliobert," or "ED-One." I had begun to work in concert with an agent in our Fort Lauderdale office to put together a conspiracy case against him. Gary, considered to be somewhat of a guru on Haitian affairs had been feverishly working toward that goal for years and was getting close to achieving it. I was optimistic enough that together we could make that happen, with him in South Florida having access to the US Attorney's Office and a Grand Jury, and me on the ground in Haiti. Gary was a very intense and tenacious agent who had interviewed countless co-conspirators of Eliobert. Those precious pieces of the larger conspiratorial puzzle consisted largely of individuals who had been arrested in the US, and subsequently provided Federal Grand Jury testimony in the Southern District of Florida, in ongoing development of the case against him. A Federal indictment of Eliobert could not be far off in the making, I thought. We just needed to link a cocaine seizure in the U.S. to him. The major obstacle after that inevitable achievement, would be getting him, somehow, to Miami. In the context of his current privileged and liberal freedoms; roaming and operating with impunity in his safe haven of Haiti, posed a huge problem to overcome.

We will revisit the riveting Eliobert story a bit later. But first and of utmost significance as it relates to all Haiti's traffickers, and ultimately the President himself and his sudden pivot from being "champion of the poor;" we need to examine the hinge on which the door swings. A dive into the case of a more notorious "Kingpin" character, in the larger scheme of the great domino dynamic, is key in this saga of the former priest and president who fell from grace.

Jacques Ketant

The most notorious of the two so designated "Kingpins" in Haiti, was Jacques Bedouin Ketant, already under indictment in the Southern District of Florida. I and others had been the recipients of many anecdotal parcels of information that Ketant had the protection of "The Palace," under the authority of the President. But it was anecdotal. Possibly no one else in Haiti had more interest in these accounts than I did because I envisioned a delicious conspiracy developing, in my mind anyway, that could change the contemporary trajectory of the country.

At some point in the mix of rapidly changing dynamics within the context of DEA's role in Haiti, after our return to our more authentic DEA selves, I saw some evidence that we were back on course. I sensed a tilt toward being able to inject a bit of trepidation into the traffickers' comfort level and cavalier, government aided routine.

One bright morning a piece of correspondence in a neatly sealed envelope arrived at our office. Enclosed was a pictorial essay of sorts. Nothing in writing of course, because cowards don't write. It was simply a couple of well-developed eight and a half by eleven-inch, colored photographs of two poor individuals who had had a drill applied to the side of their heads. The grizzly procedure had pulled brain matter from their skulls resulting in their certain death. The words "DEA Informant" inscribed on the header at the top of the glossy photographs was the intended essence of the essay at a glance. It didn't have its intended effect of intimidation, however. In fact, it had the opposite one. It demonstrated to everyone in the office that we had the bad guys on the defensive and were starting to have an impact on their collective psyche. Horribly grizzly, but a good sign, nonetheless.

With official corruption spiraling out of control, the Embassy Country Team came up with a collective, fairly novel plan for combatting it. I had been told and later came to understand, that a US visa for any Haitian who could afford to travel to the United States was worth more than gold. Not only for its status appeal but for the sense of freedom it provided and the security of those holding one for the sometimes-needed exigent escape from the country. To lose one's visa would be a catastrophic and life altering event. One person described it as a plight worse than losing one's life, which is a bit of an exaggeration I thought, but not a good thing just the same. All elements within the Embassy who could, would make credible contributions toward identifying Haitian officials involved, or benefited from the drug trafficking business, however tangential. Those so identified would have their visas revoked. The proverbial hammer came down with a hard thud.

The Team came up with a list and began to send out revocation notices with the caveat that they may be able to mitigate the revocation and help themselves by cooperating with the DEA. Brilliant, and a potential boon for us in the Port-au-Prince, DEA Country Office! I began to salivate over the potential in my recently transformed, heaven-sent DEA environment, which was offering new tantalizing possibilities and wide horizons to take in. My professional world was suddenly transformed from dust to sweet smelling possibilities of potential.

Rudy

Several days had not yet gone by when in walked the flashy and incredibly ostentatious persona of Rudy Theressan. His personality filled the space of Al's office. Rudy had a combination of charm, power of persuasion, and a masterful sense of flare. He was a character and held nothing back. Subtle could not occupy the same space as Rudy. He offered to cooperate with us, and after some getting acquainted banter, containing little substance, I told him we would be in touch very soon. After he left, Al and I just looked at each other and burst into spontaneous laughter which we could not contain. Our explosion of uncontrollable laughter continued nonstop for at least five minutes. Rudy was just too much, but did provide me with reason for optimism. I could envision the puzzle pieces for the grand conspiracy being set in their proper place, but it would require artful and graceful finesse.

The encounter with Rudy started me down a road that I never could have imagined. I sensed things were about to get wild and I felt excitement at what potential there might possibly be in store. But even if things did not fall into place as my imagination envisioned, it would still be really interesting just dealing with Rudy. This could be a wild ride. I had never encountered a personality with such cock surety and bravado in my life. Rudy may have been moved by less than angelic spirits but his personality was chalk full to the point of bursting with whatever it was; wit, charm, and not the least, cunning. The size of his persona was just as large as his larger-than-life reputation, which fell a bit on the short side of being a model of angelic behavior.

I had been told by sources over and over that Rudy was a "very bad guy," Aristide's "hit man" who was a ruthless killer that did the president's dirty work in the area of ridding him of unwanted people and problems associated with them. Aristide himself was thought of by Embassy officials to be a little off the rails in terms of his psychological balance, so such a marriage of convenience between the two was not too shocking.

I was poised to embark on an adventurous mission of some kind with a reputed ruthless killer and hit man for the President. To say this would be interesting would be an understatement. Rudy was very motivated to do something, having lost his visa and his access to the U.S. I had leverage here, the all-holy visa pitted against loyalty to the President and his protectorate. I had some challenging ideas for Rudy to prove his commitment to DEA and the U.S. Justice system so that he might earn consideration for reinstatement of his ticket to the U.S. Did I believe he could regain his travel status? I don't know, but I thought that on balance, we had to give it a try. It would take something monumental to mitigate the horrific reputation he had forged for himself, but I was eager to work with him for the sake of his rehabilitation and the potential to really shake things up in this out-of-control sea of corruption. It was worth a shot to take at the bull's eye, which is where my sights were now set.

Rudy, at the time, was the recently appointed "*Commissaire* of the somewhat mercurial and secretive police unit, "*La Brigade de Recherche et d' Intervention*" (Research and Intervention Brigade, BRI). What the research and intervention were, seemed to be up for debate, but they had a less than transparent look to them, and a suspect reputation after Rudy's appointment by the President. It was a murky appendage under the auspices of the Haitian National Police, but then again, the BRI seemed to be somewhat autonomous and independent. They were equipped and dressed like the Swat Team, but instead of the typical black uniform, and reporting structure within the HNP chain of command, the BRI wore blue and seemed not to report to anyone. The blue uniforms made them look a little less intimidating than the SWAT Team and projected a softer image, but that was far from the reality. These were special project police who seemed to have reporting obligations only to the President and likely did the dirty work for him, protecting drug traffickers, cleaning up messes that needed to be cleaned up, or eliminating those problems altogether. It was murky and Rudy was their recently installed commander, at least for a segment of the unit. Confusing and murky as the picture was, it was starting to become a bit clearer. All the while, I was paradoxically growing somewhat fond of Rudy. Life and relationships are hard to reconcile sometimes. There are constant forces tugging in opposite directions; a built-in tension with life, and this was an example. There can always be found that spark of good in even the worst acting human beings, no matter how bad; "made in the Image of God," I wanted good to happen in Rudy's heart. A project.

Ketant's Ascendancy

Beaudoin "Jacques" Ketant was responsible for smuggling tens of thousands of kilograms of cocaine into the United States from Haiti during the 1990's, rising rapidly to "Kingpin" status. When, during the late 1980's, Pablo Escobar, head of the Colombian, "Medellin Cartel," searching the Caribbean for a soft target through which to pass cocaine from Colombia into the U.S., he dominated the world's cocaine market; and he found Haiti to have the right mix of political instability, epic poverty, and bribe-hungry officials. Haiti was the choicest geopolitical and most vulnerable location in the region; being the poorest country in the Western Hemisphere, and in close proximity to the U.S. So, it was for him, the ideal transshipment location and staging point for cocaine shipments that were U.S. bound. Escobar sent his foot soldiers into Haiti to set up shop and quickly went about the business of bribing Haitian officials to monitor and guard an air strip (converted highway) outside Port-au-Prince for his drug laden planes arriving from Colombia to land on. The cartel worked directly with Lt. Col. Joseph-Michel Francois, a career soldier who in 1987, directly oversaw the security and protection of 70,000 pounds of Escobar's cocaine, destined for the United States.

As stated previously, in December 1990, Jean-Bertrand Aristide, the former charismatic Catholic priest ran for president and amassed 67 percent of the county's vote and was swept into power. He was viewed at the time as a well-intentioned reformist who likely was a threat to the drug trade. Political stability is an enemy of a thriving narco-market, so before Aristide could celebrate his first anniversary in office, he was ousted by a group of complicit military officials, including Francois, who sent him on his way to Venezuela. After the coup, Francois appointed himself as head of the National Police and installed trusted associates to key positions at the Port-au-Prince Seaport and Airport, ensuring there would be no viable obstacles to the booming cocaine business. To move loads of cocaine into the United States, Francois tapped into the services of Jacques Ketant and his network of drug runners. Ketant's inner circle consisted mostly of family and relatives. But he also established connections in the Miami neighborhood known as "Little Haiti," where many Haitian expatriates had resettled.

With the help of established connections at the Miami International Airport, Ketant was able to move suit cases packed with cocaine through the airport hassle free, by-passing Customs and security. Having effective control, Francois ensured free passage of the contraband through the airport in Port-au-Prince. Ketant and his brother, Hector, were arrested by Haitian officials in the summer of 1994, but within 24 hours were freed by Haitian police. Between 1992 and early 1995, Ketant made entry into the United States to expedite his trafficking business on at least 40 occasions. He frequented clubs in South Florida, known to be favored by drug traffickers, and leveraged his newly made connections to move drugs into expanding markets in New York and Chicago.

Ketant's cocaine trade continued to flourish throughout the 1990's, despite potential impediments, such as the death of Pablo Escobar at the hands of Colombian anti-narcotics forces; Aristides return to power in Haiti; Francois' exile to Honduras; and Ketant's contacts at the Miami airport coming under scrutiny by authorities. Not swayed, he simply redirected his efforts. By bribing a baggage handler at the JFK Airport, he began sending his couriers throughout New York City and beyond.

DEA Picking up the Scent

The DEA began to uncover evidence of Ketant's activities in Miami when seizures of cocaine were made linking him to them. Agents in Miami began to carefully and methodically construct their case against Ketant. Undercover agents infiltrated his organization and successfully began making drug buys from Ketant's distributors. He also was caught talking about killing "snitches" on a wiretap. In 1996, in New York City, DEA agents seized nine kilograms of cocaine at the JFK Airport. A suspect connected to the seizure fled in a car, then bailed out on foot before disappearing. But a briefcase in the suspect's possession was left behind in his frantic and fast footed flight from pursuing agents. Ketant's "identification" was found inside the briefcase as well as note books containing the names of other co-conspirators in his criminal enterprise. Before DEA agents could grab Ketant, he safely made it onto a plane headed to Port-au-Prince disguised as a woman.

Ketant remained safely in his refuge, that of Haiti, out of reach and out of touch of the DEA. This presented a monumental obstacle if we had any hope of ever getting him to the U.S to face drug trafficking charges; or other potential crimes such as ordering the murder of his mother-in-law in

Miami, a case in which he is still suspect. He apparently enjoyed the protection of people in high places.

Ketant was in Haiti at the moment his mother-in-law, Claudie Adam, was gunned down in broad daylight as she stepped off the sidewalk outside a shopping center in Miami, on a February morning in 1997. As she entered the cross walk, her cell phone pressed to her cheek, a masked man exited a Toyota sedan and fired at her twice. He then roared off leaving her lifeless body in the middle of the street. Claudie's son overheard Ketant screaming into her cell phone during a violent conversation with her the day before, saying he was going to kill her. While Claudie's assassination occurred as Ketant was out of reach in Haiti, he still had an established criminal organization in Miami. It has never been proven that Ketant was behind the murder, but he has remained a key suspect by law enforcement up to this day. Although the case remains open, they have never, as yet, been able to solve the murder.[1]

Indictment

In March 1997, one month after Claudie's brutal murder, a 22-count, federal indictment was handed down in the Southern District of Florida, charging Ketant, Michael-Joseph Francois and eleven other co-conspirators with drug trafficking and conspiracy. Charges included conspiracy to distribute cocaine and money laundering. DEA Special Agents painted a clear picture of Ketant's drug trafficking organization and activities in a meticulous, comprehensive case that had been scrupulously developed over many months, and finally disclosed. Informants linking Ketant to corrupt government officials in Haiti, as well as exhaustive monitoring and tracking of couriers carrying cocaine on airline flights from Haiti to Miami, and the use of wiretaps, were multiple building blocks used for the ultimate case constructed against Ketant and his organization. Despite the seamless case made against him, agents in the U.S., and Haiti for that matter, were frustrated by the lack of cooperation from the Haitian Government to arrest and extradite Ketant to the U.S.

Because of his close connections to numerous high-level corrupt government officials, Ketant remained free to run his narcotics trade in nearly plain sight, and it remained a thorn in the side of the DEA and U.S. Government interests. He had become a powerful figure in Haiti and was largely viewed as untouchable. Paradoxically, his cocaine trafficking enterprise

---

1. Timeline and events extracted from Swenson, "Rise and Fall," as well as Haitian sources.

gained even more traction and reached its highest levels ever after his indictment in the U.S.

When Ketant's cocaine smuggling enterprise, using commercial airlines hit a snag, he began secreting multiple kilograms of the drug in the hulls of maritime vessels, which were also bringing legitimate cargo into the Florida Keys and up the Miami River into Miami. His business ironically increased in a dramatic way, and so did his wealth. During my first year in Haiti, "America's Most Wanted" TV show came to Port-au-Prince to do a work-up for a future airing, featuring Jacques Ketant, The King Pin Fugitive.

21

Misplaced Hope

When Aristide had again been elected president in 2001, the hopes of many were pinned to his being Haiti's savior and reformer again, but instead his second time in office marked a period where a great run for drug traffickers began. Maybe Aristide learned from his first experience as president that ideology does not equate to worldly success and the retention of power. An accommodation with the dark side might leverage his chances for success in his desire to solidify his grip on the presidency. Surely it would be a safer bet in the current environment he inherited. And so, he apparently made the calculation, and opted for the darker side on the scale of virtue and vice, for job security, not to mention the fruits of financial gain, however rotten.

A 2001 State Department Narcotics Affairs report concluded that 15 percent of the cocaine entering the United States came through Haiti, a 25 percent increase over the previous year. That is a huge amount considering Haiti's stature among other Caribbean and Central American countries in close geographic proximity to the US. I had been in the country for two years when Aristide returned to power and it came to my attention rather quickly that he was turning a blind eye to drug trafficking at best, or was deeply complicit at worst. Both scenarios were unacceptable in my eyes.

I believed deep down I could do something about it and see to it that justice be located somewhere in this abominable situation that should not be what it had become. Fanciful and maybe unrealistic in a fallen world where dark forces are fiercely battling the good(?). Possibly, but there I was grounded in my beliefs blending into dreams of conquering those forces of evil. I felt compelled to try, bolstered by a strong dose of blind optimism which had no firm platform upon which to stand.

More shockingly, as was related to me by Obas, Ketant, the Kingpin, was named godfather to Aristide's youngest daughter and had even thrown a christening party for her! Obas knew his way around Haitian society, so I had no reason to question him. This was an amazing bit of trivia for me to wrap my head around. The pomposity of the revelation served as even more fuel poured onto the flame of determination to one day see the dominos of this absurdity begin to fall.

I reasoned that if we could somehow get Ketant to Miami to face federal drug trafficking charges there would exist a reasonable chance that he would turn on Aristide, as well as many other traffickers and corrupt officials. Because of Aristide's apparent close relationship with Ketant, I was now convinced that the President was complicit in the drug trade and was probably profiting handsomely from it. Chances were near zero that the Haitian government in its current alignment would ever, even consider cooperating with the United States with regard to extraditing Ketant. That probability was actually most likely less than zero, but somewhere in my world of believing in the impossible, I remained secure in my optimistic bubble that something would break in our favor. I believed that the brighter light of justice would break through the darkness and prevail in ultimate victory, silly as logic would carry that thought in the complex and shadowy reality that shrouded it.

I think this way of thinking as it has applied to my life and approach to things is grounded in something not readily explainable, but a sense of *feeling* that has always been my mentor, guide, and strength. A Knowing Guide, Unseen but Powerful, has taken me down ways experienced only in dreams and strong leanings of inclination. This might be called *conscience, or consciousness, or Spirit*; that quiet inner, leading voice. It can be counted on if valued and paid attention to, I sense from experience past. Just trust in it while judiciously listening carefully to its' whispers.

Opportunity Cracks the Door Open

A small crack in the window of opportunity did miraculously appear one day in May 2003, when I learned that Ketant's nephew and his teenage son beat-up another student at the Union School, a popular and favored school with diplomats and wealthy Haitians. Apparently, the nephew was involved in a romantic rivalry with the victim. Jealousy, root of many of the world's problems, escalated to violence when the nephew did not win the affections of a certain sought-after young lady in the junior romance sweep stakes. The winner of her fancy became the victim, and for this crime the poor kid was beaten by members of the Ketant family before being thrown into the trunk of a car, according to reports. He was fortunately saved by an alert and brave school security guard before a more unfortunate outcome of the potentially deadly drama could be carried out.

The victim's misfortune was potentially DEA's gain when my conniving mind went to work. I immediately envisioned a potential opportunity in the making, launched by this adolescent testosterone fueled war, turned deadly by spirits of envy and ill-will. Al, my boss, was out of the country for some reason, and I was sitting in at the 7:30: am, Country Team meeting when news of the spicy event broke. Country Team meetings are always peppered with some tidbit of catchy news, and this one woke me up at that early hour. I immediately volunteered that we might be able to use the developments to our advantage in a political and strategic way. The incident drew outrage from the diplomatic community and was a major event due to the fact that most of the school's student body were children of foreign diplomats with a sprinkling of the Haitian elite. The community was collectively appalled that their children, expected to be under the secure umbrella of diplomatic protections, were subjected to such outrageous violations of protocol in this respectable, private school. Senior diplomats at the U.S. Embassy whose very own children attended the Union School were extremely agitated. I jammed my foot into this crack in the door of opportunity!

I proposed to the Country Team that we diplomatically send a polite suggestion to President Aristide that Jacques Ketant has now become a glaring liability for his own best interests as president of Haiti. I suggested we might offer to help him out with the problem, and restore his own possibly damaged image through association, by removing Ketant from the local scene; take him to Miami to face federal narcotics and money laundering charges, thereby extricating the President from certain embarrassment caused by the incident. I conceived of a "legal" scenario where, with official Haitian authorities actually taking him into custody, we might make the argument that it was a legal arrest without any reliance on a formal extradition agreement in place, which we did not have with Haiti. This was always the stumbling block in the past; no legal means of snatching the guy. This is where I envisioned that my "newly found friend Rudy," could play a huge role. The grand idea was coming into focus but would still be very tricky to execute, and most likely would require another miracle or two to navigate the delicate situation. But those unexplainable occurrences seemed to be more visible in recent days as we moved toward an unseen destiny. The US

Embassy seemed to have bought into my plan, but remained fairly silent on the matter, so I just forged ahead, taking the absence of a "no" to mean "yes."

There was yet another monumental problem to overcome. We could not use U.S. Government/DEA resources to transport Ketant to the States, according to Embassy higher-ups. There were legal extradition issues that prohibited a clear path for that in the law, or was it just a lack of fortitude on their part? This was turning an unlikely scenario into a nearly impossible one. But I was on a role with minor miracles recently popping up all around, and with child-like bliss, I simply expected more to appear.

I was never told not to forge ahead with my scheme, but then again, maybe nobody believed it could be accomplished. After all, DEA had wanted to make this happen for years. But something in my mind was telling me: "We can do this." I just felt that it would all come together somehow, because the dynamics and myriad of unlikely moving parts seemed to be lining up in such a providential way. I could feel the momentum pushing strongly at our back toward the right outcome. I sensed the recipe for success had already been scripted and was ready to be recorded in the annuls of this particularly serendipitous moment in history. The stars looked to be aligned . . . maybe. Faith would be the key ingredient, as it always is in this life of not seeing.

I had been working on Rudy Therassan for weeks trying to convince him that what he needed to do was help me capture Ketant, if he ever had any hope of getting his U.S. visa reinstated. I now strongly suspected that Rudy worked with Ketant in his criminal enterprise and that he knew him quite well. Rudy also had a close relationship with the President based on his unique position in the National Police, and the kind of dark work he was rumored to be doing for him. Aristide had brought Rudy back to Haiti for "special projects." It became fairly obvious to me that he was a bit repulsed by my proposal because of his personal and "professional" interests, but I kept working hard to convince him that my plan was the right plan. The whole idea was averse to his closely guarded agenda, and nature, but I held out hope. Now we have Faith and Hope in the mix; earlier I told of my wish to change Rudy's heart; Love, the trifecta was complete. The relationship was a real one, but flawed from its inception. I had yet to deal with the evil and criminal components. Life is a challenge.

I was quite sure at this juncture that Rudy and his boys at the BRI had been protecting plane loads of cocaine arriving in Haiti which belonged to Ketant. If that were in fact the case, the dilemma that it presented to Rudy would certainly be a monumental and complex issue to overcome. But one day his attitude suddenly changed. It took me by surprise but played perfectly into the ongoing mysterious momentum, in a way that really left me wondering. We; the Powers above, and I, with feet on the ground, were moving this project in a forward trajectory that seemed magical and other worldly.

There were rumors flying about that the new head of the Haitian narcotics police, Evintz Brillant, had recently won favor over Rudy for the protection of Ketant's incoming cocaine shipments, and was now the man providing security for those operations. Rudy had apparently been displaced, and jarringly jilted. It might have been reasonably foreseen that Ketant found out that Rudy had been in contact with the Embassy and the DEA because of his visa revocation, and concluded that he couldn't be sure of Rudy's loyalty any longer. Crooks don't trust each other. If that were the case it would have a debilitating effect on the relationship between Ketant and Rudy, and ultimately give rise to Rudy wanting to get back at, and get revenge on Ketant. In a twist of momentous movements, Ketant needed to take out a new insurance policy on his business, which meant dropping a potential liability. Like a betrayal in a relationship between jilted lovers, this most likely had a debilitating effect on the relationship between the two, albeit a criminal one made in hell.

The twists and turns in this saga were incredible, but with each unlikely twist they seemed to twist in my favor. This ballet was in synch with the orchestra being conducted by the Maestro standing high above in the conductor's box; drawing out harmonious melodies, all the while watching the dance below, enjoying the symphonic scenario unfolding.

When I had my meetings with Rudy, we took the prudential precaution of never meeting in public. Our meetings usually took place at his home which was walled off so people could not readily see any of what was going on inside his secluded compound. It was a relatively remote place, but Haiti is like a small town in the USA where everyone knows what everyone else is doing. At any rate, Rudy had an abrupt about face in his relationship with Ketant, to my joy and rocketing excitement. Things were magically falling into place and coming together in ways I could never have engineered.

The Pilot and a Pivot

In the meantime, I had consulted with Sam, armed with his Palace connections, about the hurdle to clear regarding transportation of Ketant to Miami, if our plan worked out as we hoped. The next thing I knew a meeting had been arranged with an American pilot who doubled as a mechanic, and who auspiciously worked for the Palace as its resident pilot. I'll call him William. I initially met William at a hotel, open air restaurant not far from the airport. He seemed like a reasonable man who was himself a military veteran. He

Misplaced Hope 135

wanted to join the cause of trying to clean up the drug trafficking disaster in Haiti thereby curbing the flow of cocaine to his own country, the U.S. He had a wife and domicile in Miami but was working for the government in Haiti because it provided a lucrative income for him. There were no qualified Haitians in the country that had his skill set. He essentially commuted between Miami and Port-au-Prince on a monthly basis. This all made perfect sense to me and I was thrilled with the initial introductory exchange.

I let William in on my plan to snatch Ketant and the need to find a way to get him to Miami without using U.S. Government assets. There was some risk in divulging this audacious, secret plan to an unknown employee of the Haitian Government, but I really had no other alternative. I had a gut feeling, though, that I could trust him so I went with my instincts, combined with a prayer. William, in a smooth and confident reply stated that he wanted to help the cause and offered his services and the use of the Palace airplane. This all said with the projection of an honest and reassuring smile. The reflexive, positive response to my disclosure, led me to believe William had already been briefed on my grand plan, probably by Sam. That was fine. I trusted Sam.

I was taken aback and somewhat surprised that William could so confidently, with such surety and calm, give me the assurance that he would have the concurrence of the Haitian Government to use its assets to deliver Ketant to the States. This was essentially extraditing him without doing so. Or better yet, simply delivering him to US custody in Miami with no legal wrangling or diplomatic artistry. I couldn't have even dreamed of such a gift being delivered on this magnificent silver platter. God's hand was in this and I wasn't going to question it. Apparently, someone did get to Aristide and convinced him that he needed to divorce himself from Ketant for his own political health. We duped Aristide in another sense, in that I knew from experience that when in US custody, Ketant, the spider, would most likely quickly spin his web around the President and implicate Aristide in his sticky snare of malfeasance and corruption. I suspect that Aristide was just simply not savvy enough to envision the very long rope of American Justice and how it works. Fine with me, he was all in, it seemed.

William explained that he reported to the Chief of State Security who had similar feelings of distaste for drug trafficking and the miserable state of affairs in Haiti. William was confident he could obtain approval to use the Palace plane to transport Ketant, thus ridding themselves of the liability that Ketant had become. I don't know if this had Aristide's personal stamp of approval or not, but this was music to my ears that approached melodic sounds of profound stirrings. How all these things were falling into place was beyond my understanding, but I had faith in my dream from the beginning, and that belief was rewarded with miracles sprouting all over the wasteland of impossibilities in Haiti.

One cog in the well-oiled wheel of the emerging impossible dream from rolling along smoothly was that the Palace plane was broke. But that, I was assured by William, would be fixed. "No problem," he stated with confidence. He was working on fixing whatever was broken and was confident he could accomplish that task within two weeks. So, I had to put the brakes on the forward inclining momentum with Rudy and, wait. It might be tricky keeping Rudy engaged while waiting for William to make the plane worthy of a flight from Port-au-Prince to Miami, over the 700 nautical mile expanse of the Caribbean Sea separating the two countries. This prospect made me nervous. Rudy could be fickle. The whole atmosphere was fickle.

Tension in a Sea of Precarious Possibilities

So now it was my delicate task to keep Rudy focused on staying the course, keep his sights fixed, and stay committed to the cause. He was absolutely a critical component to the equation. He had a relationship with Ketant, and both he and Ketant had a relationship with the President. Rudy had power in his official position and also had access to the Presidential Palace which would be key in our scheme. The fluid scene of many moving parts was a complicated combination of unstable relationships that could blow up at any moment.

In the meantime, I coordinated with DEA agents in Miami so they would be on standby and have time to coordinate with the U.S. Attorney's Office there once we swung our plan into actual action. I kept Al, the DEA Country Attaché, apprised of the operation's status so he could keep the Deputy Chief of Mission and other relevant entities informed.

While we nervously waited for William to fix the Palace plane, we devised a plan for the day of executing the grand "capture." The plot, suggested by Rudy, would have him reach out to Ketant on the day of the "snatch-and-grab," and inform him the President wanted to have a meeting. This made sense at the time because of the political upheaval that had been caused by his nephew's ill-advised assault on the student at the Union School. It would be reasonable for Aristide to want to meet and talk to Ketant about that, and maybe even want to straighten things out between Ketant and Rudy. Whatever "reason" for the make-believe meeting, I deferred to Rudy's judgement on the matter. He knew them. I didn't. Rudy would then pick Ketant up and feign his intent to drive him to the Palace for the nonexistent "meeting." What actually would take place, according to the plan, would be a change of direction from the make-believe Palace destination to a run for the airport. Once there, we would neatly install Ketant onto the waiting plane and whisk him off to Miami. Simple script, but simple isn't always the way the currents flow. For now, we just had to simply wait for the plane to be repaired. Not so simple in this regard either. Great plan, not so great a circumstance. Wait, and wait, and wait some more! It made my palms sweaty.

As the days ticked off, I became increasingly nervous that Rudy would get cold feet. I kept my motivational campaign up on a daily basis, assuring him he was doing the absolute right thing for himself and for the greater good. As if he cared about the greater good, but I was making an appeal to his own greater good; and at the same time stoking his ego and attempting to inflate his self-image to that of being a hero, which he would be to me if he pulled this drama off. Maybe it all had some effect.

I also stayed in close contact with William, monitoring his progress with the plane repair project. He was also a critical figure in the grand scheme and success of the operation because he would be flying the precarious plane with its critical cargo to Miami. I was getting nervous about William getting cold feet also. When I checked in with him to get updates, he sounded a little vague about his progress, which worried me. Maybe he was intentionally dogging the whole operation. And then there was the very real possibility that someone in authority would step in with a change of heart and intervene for Ketant. I had no idea who all might be privy to this plan within the larger arena of so many corrupt individuals inserted into the bowels of the governmental system. There were a lot of tenuous, unreliable, and fragmented parts in play within this delicate scheme. I don't know what glue was holding it all together. But everyone and everything had to remain in the precarious moment of static for its success, except for the plane repair! It was a fragile confluence of synchronicity that needed divine oversight for it to work. "Please God," I prayed silently. I remained confident within an ocean of concern, however. Sweaty palms and all.

22

The Capture and The Challenge

On that momentous yet precarious day, when William assured me that the plane would be ready to go, we put our grand plan in motion. Sam and I drove to Rudy's house shortly before noon. We met in Rudy's sprawling bedroom/living room which was well furnished, unlike the rest of the lavish home. Decorations and artifacts in the complicated room were eerie and presented a violent theme to the decor. Knives on the walls and guns laying all around. The room had an element of voodoo imagery which made it all a little uncomfortable for my taste, but then again, Rudy was alleged to be a bit of a violent human being, so the trappings were not out of character for him. I just accepted that this was Rudy and his portrait. He maintained his vibrance and his durable gift to charm and plant his huge persona in the midst of space and dominate it, but he was a bit more reserved in this particular moment. He instinctively knew, I believe, that he was about to set off an explosion that would send out reverberations beyond his own imagination. He poured himself a glass of whisky and lustily gulped it down before placing the call to Ketant.

Rudy was instantly back in character when talking to Ketant on the phone. Although he was speaking in Creole, he sounded very much in control and dominating the moment, as he told Ketant that Aristide wanted to see him at the Palace and informed him he was coming over to pick him up. This scenario had a ring of reasonableness to it because Rudy was an official of the Government and would naturally have access to the Palace, whereas Ketant did not. So, picking him up in a government vehicle made perfect sense. I was straining to gage the success of his argument based on the tone of his voice.

The call lasted longer than what seemed it should and I began to question whether Ketant was buying into the ruse, or maybe not. Apparently, they were negotiating about Ketant bringing his security people along with him. Rudy's power of persuasion was impressive because he talked Ketant into coming by himself and leaving his security cadre where they were. Our plan had now been launched and we were out of the starting blocks, fast, running full speed into the eventful day, and beyond. Rudy departed without hesitation with one of his own security devotees while Sam and I stayed at the house to wait his return, hopefully with Ketant in hand. Hope here was a major part of my consciousness.

They returned a short while later, Ketant in flex cuffs (plastic handcuffs). Rudy had apparently convinced him that he needed to be handcuffed as a matter of Palace visitor protocol as it applied to murderers, drug traffickers and all-around persons of ill repute. Ketant did not resist, in a likely, instant flash of conscience awareness, but he had to start feeling a little suspicious at that point, I thought. I reached out to William to advise him that the mission was "a go," and that we had Ketant in custody. He replied that he needed about two more hours to get the plane fixed. This put me into a mild panic, and a sick feeling of anxiety quickly invaded my physiology and mental well-being. I took a deep breath and tried hard to suppress those uninvited and unwanted awful feelings. "Remain calm," I silently screamed to myself. It was hard given the fragility of our operation.

The thought of keeping Ketant squirreled away from anyone and under control while maintaining the secrecy of our mission loomed as a daunting undertaking. The situation with the plane just didn't seem right and all kinds of nightmarish, panicky thoughts began invading my consciousness. Was someone trying to sabotage our plan? I didn't really know William that well and therefore did not have a reliable history with him to lean on. My confidence in him was beginning to wane. I wanted to believe he would come through, as he continued to project a measure of reassurance that he would be ready to go before too long. This put us in the very uncomfortable position of having to drive around the outskirts of Port-au-Prince, keeping our distance from people, with a very bad and unpredictable hombre in the back seat of Rudy's car.

Sam and I were following in my car, not knowing if or when we would be ambushed by other very bad people in an effort to liberate Ketant. All the myriad ugly possibilities were hard to keep at bay and from invading my imagination. I struggled to stay composed and prepared, for whatever could happen, but again I just silently said "please God." Simple, but that is all I could mutter in the moment.

The minutes seemed like hours as they ticked by at a trickle and I prayed silently, as well as I could focus on that mental activity. I invoked my spiritual friend, St. Joseph for protection and help. He did a good job doing that for Jesus when he was a child, and had been a spiritual companion throughout my career. Maybe he would hear me now. I intermittently called William to get updates on the status of his work on the plane. If the plane was still not flight worthy, why on God's green earth had he not informed me before we kidnaped Ketant, putting us in this horribly precarious position? I was growing more than a little mystified and irritated.

Rudy kept assuring Ketant that the meeting with Aristide was still on, but that he was busy with presidential stuff and would send word to Rudy when he was ready to see him. As powerful at persuasion as Rudy was, I wondered how long he could keep Ketant in the mindset of belief he was still waiting to see the President. It had now been hours since Rudy picked him up. He apparently was doing an adequate job, but this could not go on for much longer before any logical human being would figure out that something was terribly amiss.

Storm Clouds Hovering

As the afternoon dragged on seeming like eternity, the skies turned an ominous eerie green color, which turned my apprehensive mood to an even darker one. We drove to a remote area outside the city, which Sam pointed out was historically an area where the bodies of political enemies and other assassinated victims were dumped. It had a name associated with Voodoo that I don't recall, but that bit of information darkened my mood even more. Sam's history lesson got me more worried about what might be going on in Rudy's head. With his reputation I didn't know what to think he might be planning to do. Thoughts started to creep into my brain that he could just decide to shoot Ketant, eliminate him, and be done with the situation altogether. He could make a flimsy claim of self-defense. Why would that be out of character for him with his reputation? I had no answer to my question. Logic informed me that it would be a reasonable solution for him in the moment, and my anxiety level reached uncharted territory. I did not want to be any part of a murder scenario. It was becoming worrisome and the sounds of cymbals clashing in my moral hearing senses were clanging at untenable levels. I did not want to hear that sound.

At one point, Rudy pulled off to the side of the road, got out of his car, and approached my vehicle. He spoke to me through my rolled down window, emotionally expressing serious doubt about going through with our plan. He suggested that we just cancel the operation and Ketant would not be the wiser, having yet no real clue what we were up to. If we just let him go, I thought, we would have forever lost the chance of ever getting him to the States to face justice. I was not about to give up, and I told Rudy that he was doing a great service for the United States of America, stroking his ego again. Besides, he needed to get this done in order to get his visa reinstated. I told him the plane would be ready in minutes. Apparently, my power of persuasion was not too shabby either; because Rudy took a deep breath, cinched up his pants, threw out his chest and instantly got his mojo back intact. He said: "Okay Dave, we'll do it." Catastrophe averted(!), for a few more precious minutes.

Now it was beginning to get dark with heavy storm clouds taking over the Haitian skies. I was informed by William that he'd given up on fixing the Palace plane but he did have a plan B. Thank you Lord! There happened to be a much smaller plane available, designed for much lessor challenges than flying to Miami from Haiti, adding to the bizarre circumstances of our more than bizarre drama being played out. The plane belonged to someone he knew and William was given the privilege of borrowing it for a day or two. How do things like that happen, I asked myself; but asked William no questions, just grateful that he had a plan B. I was just desperate at this point and had no time, or energy left to insert more time delaying inquiries. But the little Cessna, which he said he thought could make it to Miami, was available to him. He though it could make it? That sounded far from confident, but by that point I would have settled for a canoe to paddle Ketant to Miami. Another little miracle popping up, "maybe."

Get this Nightmare Airborne

Obas and Herman, from my office, met us at the airport. It was now dark with heavy storm clouds in the night sky, making for a successful unfolding of this unlikely scenario seem even more ominous and treacherous, with a pinch of gloom added to the mixture. It did not look like optimal conditions for a night flight of over 700 miles in stormy weather to Miami, in a tiny Cessna that the pilot "thought could make it" in better conditions. No backing out now. We had come too far and our commitment had reached irretractable levels. Rudy told Ketant that they were going to fly a government helicopter to the Palace for security reasons, which he apparently believed because he was still surprisingly compliant. I cannot imagine how many lies Rudy had to make up over the many hours of having Ketant in the back seat of his car, for him to be willing to still go along with the incredible charade.

But it was, up to this point, apparently still working. Ketant allowed Rudy to help him climb into the helicopter. I was amazed and impressed at what a great con man Rudy was. I was, at the time just fine with that; in fact, I was grateful for his less than virtuous qualities in that particular moment. William readied the Cessna for its voyage over the sea and through the storm clouds, and was parked just off the runway about 100 yards away from where we were in the helicopter hangar.

Just a few minutes went by before things suddenly got very crazy. When Rudy removed Ketant from the helicopter, the electrons in his brain apparently began firing correctly, alerting him to the fact that he was in fact not going to the Palace for a meeting with the President. The little plane on the runway was very visible and did not look normal sitting there poised for takeoff. Ketant suddenly woke up to the reality that something else, unwelcomed, was occurring. And as Jesus warned Peter, "People will take you where you do not want to go," Ketant was now having his Jesus moment. He saw the Cessna warming up and did not like the looks of that picture.

Suddenly he bolted with lightning speed, looking more like Jamaican, world championship sprinter Hussein Bolt, catching us all by surprise. I was amazed at how fast the skinny guy in handcuffs could run. Now it made sense that when being chased by police in New York, and ditched his car to escape on foot years earlier, he was successful. He was not handcuffed then and had abandoned his briefcase full of incriminating evidence to give his speed even more advantage. Even now with handcuffs on his wrists he showed impressive quickness and agility, so much so that I was left standing with my jaw dropped. I was a runner in my day but never a sprinter. I didn't even consider that I could catch him. Luckily Herman had the gift of swiftness also, his cousin a wide receiver in the NFL; and he took off after Ketant, closely following him into an open-door structure where Herman was able to corral him in the restrictive confines of the building.

Back in our now more cautious control, we carefully escorted Ketant to, and securely onto the plane; Herman and Obas on either side of him, eliminating any possibility of him being able to escape again. Once he was securely seated in the plane, in that very precious moment of relief, I breathed a deep, sweet, luscious breath of the night time air. I would not feel entirely at ease, however, until I saw the wheels of the tiny aircraft lift off the tarmac. My paranoid inclined mind was telling me that there was still the chance that Ketant's liberators could come screaming onto the scene and stop the little plane that "thinks it can." So, we waited and watched.

After watching the long, slow, anxiety packed, taxi to the far end of the runway; the plane turned toward us gradually picking up speed, at what seemed like a snail's pace, and eventually lifted off the ground, inch by inch. These little planes do not move fast. When I saw the separation of the plane's wheels from the tarmac, I instantly felt the enormous weight of anxiety escape from my head to my toes. I never felt so relieved in my life. I turned to Sam and Rudy, and said: "We did it." Rudy departed, understandably exhausted from his very stressful day, while Sam and I drove across the street to the new Shell gas station, adjacent to the airport. There we bought a couple beers and stepped outside to drink them in celebratory relief. There we stood and basked in our success and reminisced about the day's nerve racking, but ultimately wonderful events. It was one of those very satisfying moments after overcoming enormous obstacles, where bliss sweeps in to replace vice gripping stress, which had dominated the perspective all day long. Indeed, all was well in that moment shared with Sam outside the Shell convenience store.

The Smell of Sweet Success

The next day I received a call from Obas, still in Miami, while I was at the office. In his typical Haitian, booming, animated voice he bellowed: "Dave, I've never been so afraid in my (expletive) life on that flight to Miami in that (expletive) plane." They had flown through some vicious stormy weather on their way north and the little Cessna got tossed around pretty severely. On top of that, the plane's fuel gage was on empty as they made their approach to the Miami International Airport. Obas thought they were going to die, justifiably so. I apologized for the harrowing experience but was elated at the success of the impossible mission. Obas was no stranger to helping out on high profile missions. In 1989 he escorted dictator Manuel Noriega from Panama to the U.S. after his indictment on drug trafficking charges in the U.S., and subsequent ouster from Panama.

What made our Ketant event so sweet was that he had expressed to Obas, on their frightful trip to Florida, his desire to talk and to tell all. I had banked on that being the case all along and thought it would likely happen, but it did surprise me that Ketant made known his intention to Obas so early on. Usually, defendants require the process of prolonged negotiations and time to digest how much trouble they are facing before they offer to cooperate. Ketant must have been thinking about this for some time. I guess he knew he was cooked from the moment he was put on that brave little Cessna in Port-au-Prince. Or he had a "come to Jesus" moment, and like Obas, thought he was going to die on the way.

Adding to the brightness of the picture, from my perspective at least, it would most likely herald the end of Aristide as president. With Ketant unleashed, I could envision more than the undoing of Aristide and his presidency, but also the demise of numerous other high-level drug traffickers in Haiti. This auspicious day, after the harrowing one we all had experienced, would send shock waves of tsunami proportions through that Caribbean Island country; with Ketant spewing dirt and truth, describing the world he so influenced in Haiti. Dreaming again, momentarily, I thought it may be a harbinger of a new beginning once again for Haiti. A severe disruption in the insidious narco-political marriage of drugs and politicians. It was truly a coup of enormous proportion for the good guys, which would likely have significant impact on the political dynamic of the country, for the better . . . for the time being.

23

Fall Out from Folly

In Miami Ketant would now face the 1997 indictment which he had eluded for almost a decade. He confessed to having smuggled 30 tons of cocaine to the United States from Haiti in a reduced plea agreement and was sentenced to 27 years in federal prison. He also was to forfeit $15 million in reparations. At the time of sentencing Ketant went off on a 25-minute diatribe aimed at Federal Judge Federico Moreno, according to the *New York Times*. Calling out Aristide, Ketant raged: "The man is a drug lord. He controlled the drug trade in Haiti. He turned the country into a narco-country."

"I'm not sentencing President Aristide," Moreno said from the bench. "He hasn't been charged."

"Not yet your honor," Ketant replied. "You will be seeing him pretty soon."[1]

That was precisely and deliciously what I had dreamed of and hopefully expected to hear from Ketant about Aristide. It was music playing wonderful melodic themes of resolution and truth. The President's days would be numbered now and Haiti would be better off for it. I liked looking at that big picture, a success in my vision of the country, and the drug trafficking world in general. Successful mission by way of grace and effort, I suppose is the way to view it, and to simply appreciate the outcome. I did.

When Ketant's world finally did come crashing down, visible images representing his amassed wealth were conspicuous. There were millions of dollars' worth of assets; a hill-top mansion in a posh Port-au-Prince

---

1. Swenson, "Rise and Fall."

neighborhood decorated with white Mediterranean columns and elegant fountains from which water gracefully cascaded. The walls inside the mansion were draped with 200 expensive, high-quality paintings, one of which was a Monet, valued at $1 million. Later, inside a safe $4 million US, in cash was discovered. A Hummer H-2 and a Cadillac Escalade, parked in his driveway, had been a routine part of the normal scenery.

A snapshot of the opulent corruption on the island in the Caribbean run amok, in the midst of the prevailing, prominent, reality of abject poverty familiar to the vast majority of its citizenry, is an appalling concept to reconcile. A moral outrage heaped on top of an illegal one.

More Rudy, More Drama

Early in the day, two days following the capture of Ketant, while driving to the Embassy, I received a call from Rudy. He informed me that he was on his way over to the home of Hector Ketant, Jacques' younger brother, who I knew by now was complicit in and assisted with Jacques' trafficking enterprise. Rudy said he was going to arrest Hector. Now Rudy was on a roll, but I reasoned that he needed to do something to mitigate the Hector factor who would certainly be seeking retaliation for Jacques' unforeseen, unexpected, and unimaginable arrest. Hector had a quite well-established reputation for being ruthless himself, more so even than Jacques, and allegedly played the role of serving as Jacques' enforcer, including killing suspected informants and other undesirables.

I reasoned that Hector would likely try to avenge his brother's capture and would be seeking to do Rudy some serious harm at some point in time. That was just simply Haitian justice. Rudy's intent was probably an attempt to preempt that scenario by being proactive and getting to Hector first. In Rudy's world of logic, that was the only sensible thing to do. I was not confident that this encounter was going to end up looking as through a lens of roses and light, or in some gentlemanly negotiated truce of some kind.

I told Rudy to be careful and to call me at the conclusion of his operation. He assured me he would. Did I like the scenario? Not really. But it was out of my control, which was no control. I submitted to the rightful purveyor of decision making in that moment, to make the call in his own wild world of survival.

A couple hours later I received the second call of the day from Rudy. I was anxious to take this one. In a surprisingly calm voice, he said: "Dave, I shot and killed Hector. He went for his gun when I tried to arrest him." I said: "Are you alright?" and he responded that he had been shot in the arm but it was just a scratch and he was fine. I envisioned an old fashion Western shoot out taking place at Hector's house. Why was I not surprised at the outcome with that kind of toxic, volatile alchemy in that untamed jungle of self-preservation? Both these guys had pretty violent reputations. Rudy took photographs of the scene and later showed them to me. Sure enough, Hector was very dead, lying in a pool of blood along with two of his gangster buddies who were pretty shot up also, and also pretty dead. Nobody was surprised at this outcome.

The Aftermath

I spent the next couple weeks lobbying Embassy officials to reinstate Rudy's visa as his just reward for his valiant and bold work in the capture of Jacques Ketant. At first, they balked, which disturbed me, because the result of his cooperation was about to change the political landscape in Haiti, and he had stuck his head way out there to get the job done. But then again, maybe I was the only one in the building who viewed the scenario from that perspective. I had invested a lot to assure Rudy that with Ketant's arrest he likely could regain his visa status, and to a large extent I believed that to be the case. Ideological naivete maybe. But I also argued that DEA agents in Miami, as well as the prosecutors in the U.S. Attorney's Office wanted to debrief Rudy, in so far as he could provide valuable information into on-going investigations with a Haitian nexus in the U.S.

Apparently, my argument worked, in part. Rudy was granted a temporary visa to travel to the U.S. for interviews and debriefings. He was ecstatic, but I explained to him that he would have to cooperate fully if he wanted to turn his temporary status into a longer term one. Rudy seemed fine with that and made plans to travel to Miami. I also traveled to Miami while Rudy was there and met with him once by design and once by chance at the Miami Airport when I incidentally ran into him near the International Terminal. On that occasion he gave me a demonstrative hug, which was Rudy's typical way of expressing himself; on a big stage, emotive, boisterous and exuberant. The kind of greeting only Rudy could give, but it was vintage Rudy. I laughed and hugged him back. My wife was with me and knew Rudy's reputation but she didn't seem impressed, just a minor chortle in response to his Grammy worthy emotivism. He was genuinely grateful for the reestablishment of his access to the States and was expressive of that, but this would not be the end of his complex story.

The Web Widens

It was obvious that Rudy had a new lease on life with his regained freedom, having open ended passage to the United States once again. I think he felt he needed to hide out in Miami for a while after taking out both Jacques, and in a more permanent way, Hector Ketant, within a two-day time frame. There would be people in his world on the island country who would want to exact revenge on him for turning off the spigot of their lucrative income flow.

I had an uneasy feeling, but kept it to myself, that with Ketant most likely telling all he knew, about everyone he knew in the world of drug trafficking, Rudy himself would wind up in his snare. Sure enough, Rudy's newfound freedom came to an abrupt halt when DEA agents in Miami saw fit to seek his indictment, with Ketant's cooperation, and take him into custody. I was disappointed for him, but not surprised. Rudy had done some bad things in Haiti, yet I had developed an affinity for him and was genuinely grateful for what he had done for the cause, with regard to Ketant. Also, with his pivotal help, the dominoes of corruption began to fall, rapidly. He stuck his neck way out there to capture a featured "America's Most Wanted Fugitive," risking his own life in the process. But justice is justice, and in the end, he was left to answer for his own iniquities. I just felt bad for him, for his own misguided sake and folly.

A week or so after Rudy's arrest, his distraught girl friend called me. She told me that Rudy was despondent and wanted to kill himself. I told her that I had not been involved with his arrest and didn't know the details but would make sure the appropriate people in Miami were fully aware of the help he provided us. And I did. I made calls to the DEA there, and the U.S Attorney's Office, but in the end, they had to do their job as best seen fit. Justice is what it is, while the system tries very hard to discern that difficult and complex concept. Ultimately, the finality of justice is up to that Higher Power, more than what we ourselves are able to dispense. So, in the meantime, we just do our best.

That was the last of any interaction I had with Rudy Theressan. But the wild memories he left me with have stayed with me through time; because of his one-of-a-kind giant personality, and the wild ride we took, are unforgettable. To this day I chuckle to myself when recalling his grand entrance into Al's office years before, dressed like a mobster character out of a 1940's mafia movie.

Rudy pled guilty in Federal Court, in the Southern District of Florida, in April 2004, to one count of conspiracy to import more than twenty kilograms of cocaine into the U.S. Six other counts were dropped as a result of the plea agreement. He was sentenced to 15 years in federal prison which was later reduced to 10 years for his cooperation and testimony in convicting other Haitian and Colombian narcotics traffickers. He admitted to my fellow DEA agents that he provided security for the off-load of multiple tons of cocaine from planes as they arrived from Colombia, landing on that shiny, modern highway on the outskirts of Port-au-Prince.

Sorry Rudy, and thanks for the help, but that's what justice looks like when you follow the career path you chose. Best wishes.

24

Eliobert, Kingpin Round Two

As I briefly mentioned earlier, there was a concurrent, ongoing project that I had been working on for some time. From almost the day I arrived in Haiti I had been hearing reports about the most potentially prolific trafficker on the Island of Hispaniola. Jean Eliobert Jasme, known locally simply as "Eliobert," was cloaked in a much different image than Jacques Ketant. Where violence was associated with Ketant, Eliobert, a major trafficker on par with Ketant, was a businessman and benefactor, of sorts, to the community. He used his profits from drug trafficking to undertake community projects that helped people. An ironic blend of illegality and doing good for his brethren, a rare concept; in the mold of a "Robinhood" in the drug trafficking world where violence and greed are more the norm.

I had been working with an agent, Gary, out of the Fort Lauderdale District Office, on advancing a case in our mutual investigation into Eliobert's trafficking activities. Eliobert was alleged to be at the top of the trafficker heap among Haitian traffickers, in terms of volume, at the time. Gary had been methodically putting together a case against him for a number of years, so he and I joined forces by way of our mutual interest in him as a natural consequence. There were also co-conspirators and potential witnesses in custody, in Florida, who had shown signs of willingness to provide testimony, stingy as it was, about Eliobert's trafficking activities. The missing piece, however, was tying a seizure of cocaine to him. Or perhaps some potent testimony from our very recent advocate in the person of Jacques Ketant. The two may have even cooperated with each other on occasion.

Eliobert, the well-known business man in Haiti enjoyed legitimate success. He owned a cement factory and construction business. He operated in the open without the burdensome image of being a notorious criminal; and because of his substantial benevolent contributions (presumed by me to be bribes disguised as donations, but cynicism comes with the territory) he moved about Port-au-Prince freely, unencumbered with the concern he might be arrested, at least not by Haitian officials. Eliobert had a swagger and projected a huge presence in his own right.

Another Spring in the Fall?

The blockbuster benefit that emerged from the Ketant epic family misstep at the Union School and the ultimate tumble of Jacques into his own self woven web of undoing, was what he would do with the predicament he was embroiled in. He had some control to salvage the rest of his life, or at least part of it, with the U.S. Justice system's justice on sale, "Fall" event. He had a lot of goods to sell and could choose to cooperate and mitigate his bleak future of time spent behind bars. Ketant suddenly found himself under enormous pressure to cooperate with the DEA and Justice Department, for the sake of salvaging some of his future free time on this earth. That opportunity coupled with the wealth of knowledge, within his personally owned space in the dark and murky world of drug trafficking, could improve his situation substantially. He knew this. Ketant, it seemed, had already decided to talk and talk and talk some more. Good move from my perspective.

Ketant had the potential to break open the whole Haitian drug trafficking scene in a way that could not have been imagined prior to his arrest. There suddenly emerged existential exigency, exploding in the heads of those of his same ilk. A serious and sober calculation of their own liability, in the context of the potential threat he posed, was suddenly required as a result of his sudden and unexpected arrest. This dynamic alone would prove to be a boon to my own agenda in Haiti.

Ketant could most likely link seizures of cocaine made in the U.S. to certain high level traffickers, in addition to the mountains of intelligence he could provide about them, thereby laying the ground work for countless high-profile conspiracy cases to be constructed. In short, Ketant's arrest was a gold mine for DEA agents and others in their efforts to develop new investigations and make cases, targeting Haitian-U.S. cocaine trafficking operations. Additionally, he could, with certainty and specificity, identify Haitian governmental complicity, which had been a thorn in our side for too long. It was the powerful, intangible dynamic flying under the radar of

Ketan's high profile arrest that I had hoped for; and it scared the wits out of traffickers in Haiti, and those with Haitian connections. The status quo and comfort level among them had vanished, literally overnight on that perilous flight to Miami.

I was hearing what the effects and fallout from Ketant's capture were from various sources. It had shaken up that particular world and put it on its heels. In our corner of the planet, those in the drug trade were all now feeling vulnerable. Up to this point they had been collectively feeling fairly smug about their shield of protection covering their nefarious activities.

This existential, psychological, and political shift would serve me well with the Eliobert project and beyond. Sources told me Haitian traffickers were running scared and laying low. Ketant's capture and his brother's demise at the hand of Rudy's guns, had them psychologically thrown off balance. The vulnerability they felt in the aftermath of a notorious Drug Kingpin being captured and whisked off to the U.S., left them not sure at all what their own fate might look like, or what might be divulged about them. They suddenly sensed a very real, present danger. Those in the dark trade had to shift their mind-set for the possibility they would be compromised and find themselves in dire need of an insurance plan for leveraging their own footing. The perfect psychological stage to manipulate the power of paranoia was set.

Act Two: The Heavy Curtain Opens

Within the rapidly changing Haitian drug trafficking environment, another serendipitous moment emerged with perfect timing. In yet another instance of gold discovered in the mining project of the Embassy's visa revocation program targeting suspected drug traffickers, there suddenly appeared an individual who I will refer to as Gasby. He contacted me and wanted to meet. Gasby, somewhat sheepishly, divulged he had a lot of information to disclose about the Haitian drug trade and was inclined to share it. It was obvious to me that he was both feeling the Ketant factor; as well as the visa revocation pressure, and was quite scared, of everything, it seemed. Gasby was extremely fearful of losing his U.S. visa, rightly so; and wanted to protect it by hedging his bet in advance, by talking. Furthermore, he wanted to secure a visa for his wife. Now that he was switching loyalties, to the side of the DEA, he and his family's safety might surely be in some jeopardy. Good guess Gasby. This is Haiti we're living in, not the land of Oz.

He was one of those who felt vulnerable because of the tsunami set off by the Ketant event, and the visa revocation program which caused the shift in tectonic plates, causing the earthquake before the tsunami. What had been Gasby's predictable world had suddenly shifted off its center of gravity. Of all the traffickers in Haiti who had previously been identified and known to us, Gasby's name was missing. I had never heard of him. He was a new character to me in the Haitian trafficker context. This was probably due to his somewhat lower ranking among the more notorious Haitian traffickers. But as it turned out, I later learned from my more reliable intelligence sources, Gasby was a player. He was just able to stay under the radar more so than some others because of the role he carved out for himself in the trade.

Gasby's niche in the over-all scheme of things, I learned, was the infinitely less visible vocation of operating as a maritime navigator, smuggling cocaine from Haiti to the Bahamas on smaller commercial fishing vessels. From there, recreational sailing vessels would complete the smuggling route up into Fort Lauderdale and other smaller East Coast, Florida points of entry. The reason Gasby was not better known to us was because he had a layer of relative safety built into his more modest scheme. He didn't venture into smuggling drug loads directly into the U.S. Of course, his chosen role to play would be far less lucrative for him, but also with much reduced exposure to U.S. law enforcement. Gaspy was a "play it safe" kind of guy, I would painfully come to realize from many subsequent encounters, demanding plenty tests of my patience. A virtue, I have come to discover.

The Golden Gasby Connection

Gasby knew many of the players in the maritime trafficking business, but there was one person he was connected to that I was intensely interested in, that being Eliobert. Delightfully, shocking my cognitive sensibilities, Gasby disclosed one day that his wife was Eliobert's cousin. Probably a misstep in his calculations to divulge that, but they were very stimulating rhythms to the drum beat of my thought process. Gasby had a closer relationship to Eliobert than I would have initially ever imagined. This information sent waves of exhilarating, electrical pulses, tearing into my imagination as to what potential there might be here.

Gasby was much better than a "potential" conduit to Eliobert, that up to this point I could only dream of. He was the conduit! I could enlist his help if I crafted a strategy correctly and carefully. Because of his familial relationship with him, Gasby seemed to think I would give him a pass on targeting Eliobert in any sort of way. He was wrong, very wrong. He didn't know it yet, but I was going to take advantage of this gift of manna without having to sully him up, much at all.

Well, the revelation did seem heavenly, and I did take a glance in that direction, in amazement at how all these fortuitous things could be happening after the arid beginning of my desert time in Haiti four years earlier. It didn't make things easier, just more fun, with help from the strong downwind rush of air into my front sail, the chute.

I had to spend countless, frustrating hours trying to convince Gasby that he needed to cooperate with me, completely. I pounded the drum beat that he needed to harvest some sorely lacking courage if he wanted to protect his U.S. visa. I was totally focused on Eliobert now, and didn't really care what he had to offer about other guys in the business.

Gasby, unlike Rudy, the ruthless and reckless, was very timid and fearful despite his large physical stature. He was a mountain, borderline Haitian giant of a man with the courage of a butterfly. I was trying to rectify in my mind how a guy can take such risks trafficking drugs, and not be able to step up in the right ways. Easy money and greed, I suppose. It trumps courage and virtue for some. They all purchased their predicament, however; while reaping large false profit, not facing the truth of what they had purchased. Cowardly, when finally having to face the light, and truth, at the end of the day.

The Gasby project was going to require finesse and a boatload of patience. Both he, Rudy, and others told me that Eliobert was laying very low in the wake of the Ketant upheaval. I had to wait for the magical moment, and one more little smidgen of help from the Divine Supervisor of Investigations, above.

A Breakthrough in the Breakdown of Normal

After four years of working in concert with DEA in New York, Miami, and Fort Lauderdale, secret indictments of Eliobert were at last handed down from the US Southern District of New York, and Southern District of Florida, in Miami. I was jubilant and very energized at the possibility of engineering his capture and somehow getting him to the U.S. to face charges in these indictments.

Rudy was now useless in any possible contrived scheme to lure Eliobert into the daylight after what he had already notoriously done with Ketant. He was pretty much a burned-up commodity in that regard. He had been well worth the expenditure for what he had already accomplished, many times over. Rudy's debt had been paid in full, according to my accounting. Drug traffickers would now, however, be strongly inclined to stay miles clear of him. I finally came up with an idea that I thought was crazy, but just might work, within the context of the current socio-psycho mindset that had most likely infiltrated the minds of those who comprised that particular segment of Haitian society; the drug trafficking sub-set.

The idea of sending a message to Eliobert, somehow, to set up a meeting to discuss our mutual cooperation in order to, in essence, give him a degree of cover, seemed like the best shot at getting our hands on him. A rather unorthodox approach, I thought, but one that could possibly work given the current upended state of affairs in their unorthodox world. I had an irrational confidence in my upside-down plan, even though I shouldn't have. It just might work, a voice screamed inside my head, crazy as it sounded at the same time.

My thought was to reverse the natural order of adversarial attitudes between cops and those who break the law, a most natural mindset, like darkness and light. Flip the natural tendency, was the idea. If I reached out to Eliobert with a positive message, given the current climate, he just might bite. I needed to get the message to him that I was willing to offer him day light by being an advocate, if I had any hope of meeting him face to face. The messaging had to be right. In order to ultimately make face to face contact with him I had to make him feel as though it was to his advantage to meet. Delicacy was paramount, and the right approach required, if I had any inkling of hope of pulling this unlikely scenario off. After all, he surely knew of Rudy's reputation; and the fact that by cooperating with me, by all appearances anyway, things worked out well for him. Rudy was currently in Miami. That sent a statement by itself. Another potent, not so subtle argument for reinstating Rudy's visa. I had to act on Eliobert while that still appeared to be the case because it may not remain looking so good for Rudy too much longer.

Timing here was critical. Subtle and sneaky? Yes, but that is precisely what is required at times in the messy world of fighting crime, in the attempt to reconcile darkness to the light. Dirty work in a fallen world, but taking a page from the devil's playbook, chicanery has to sometimes be temporarily borrowed from his own tool box.

There has always been a feeling of tension for me when scheming criminals. The tension is borne by some mild remorse; duping them and being dishonest, to their personal detriment on the one hand; mixed with a feeling of exhilaration, because I was doing God's work, and what was right on the other. Conscience be my guide; the latter always won the argument. Besides it was fun . . . and my job.

25

The Mountain, the Smoke and the Fire

With my rather unorthodox strategic plan, I figured I could pull Gasby over his personal mountain of trepidation, and give him cover with plausible deniability. He would simply relay the message to Eliobert that I wanted to talk to him and then provide him my phone number. There would be no threat posed to Eliobert by just talking to me on the phone, and Gasby could claim his innocence in doing nothing more than just relaying an innocuous message. His role in the matter would appear totally clear of dubious intentions other than the fact that he was talking to me. In the current climate though, even that wouldn't look too out of the ordinary. Everyone was looking for an advantage. It would then be incumbent upon me to lure Eliobert out of the woods to meet me face to face, for his own perceived advantage. A perfect plan, possibly, but a long shot at making it work. Part of the psychology, I reasoned, rested in him believing in his own invincibility, built on his life's work building his reputation and security within institutions of officialdom inside Haiti's government; in addition to operating on his home field. Besides all that to factor into the complex scheme, Eliobert was probably a little confused, as were many within Haiti's drug trafficking circles. The criminal institution had been turned on its head with the arrest of Ketant. Nobody knew what to expect after that, so what was there to lose? So many moving parts and so much to consider. I thought Eliobert might bite.

Amazingly, Gasby came through and did his part by simply delivering the message. Now all I could do is wait and hope that the upheaval in Haiti's drug trafficking circles, and Eliobert's psychological state of mind would merge into some sort of agreeable alignment, nudging him toward an interest in at least talking to me. I was confident now.

I waited for a day or two, or three, and then the call came. "Hello." "This is Eliobert. How are you?" I asked. "I'm fine," said with calm and easy confidence, surprising and encouraging to hear. More encouraging was that he sounded comfortable engaging with me. Now we could deal, I thought. He seemed to be in the right frame of mind, giving me an assuring sense that we could talk within a context that made enough sense to him to do so with manageable risk. He was certainly intrigued enough to have responded to my invitation. It was a good sign to say the least. "We need to meet and have a conversation," I said to him. I can't really recall all the details of our conversation on the phone, but we spoke for a minute or two and agreed to talk by phone again in a few days. The way in which the conversation played out, and the general tone of it, left me feeling optimistic that we could eventually have a face-to-face meeting. I had to be extremely delicate with this initial interaction, but felt very satisfied with it afterward. This is where tension comes into play. From our short, initial encounter, there was aroused in me a sense that we could grow to like each other, but I was setting him up for a fall.

Eliobert did call me back after a few days, and during that conversation, I somehow convinced him it was in his best interest to meet with me and talk about the general state of drug trafficking in Haiti, a subject he was an expert on, me being his student. That was a vague pitch, but amazingly he bought it. We agreed to talk again in a few days to establish a time and place for a face-to-face meeting. My heart started beating faster, and maybe there was even a grin on my face at the conclusion of the call, but there was no one near me to see it.

Now I had to scramble to coordinate the logistics of the meeting; how we would take Eliobert into custody, and the transportation issues we had to deal with. This time around, most likely because of our success with the Ketant case, and the production we were getting from his cooperation, the Embassy brass, from the top down, were willing to support this operation. I had no idea what the Haitian Government's position would be on the issue; but Sam, my official government conduit, was onboard, and he either had the blessing of Aristide or he didn't care what the President thought. I never asked.

The U.S. Coast Guard Air Wing, in Miami, through the coordination and efforts of our own Liason Officer, Captain Mike, offered to fly down to Port-au-Prince and transport Eliobert to South Florida. The only caveat was, we were to have Eliobert in custody before they would launch their plane from Miami. This was all joyful news to my ears! Actual American support with American assets! The Coast Guard plane would be standing by ready to take off immediately upon getting word that Eliobert was in custody. This was shaping up to be an immensely smoother operation than the Ketant fiasco. How we managed this diplomatically, I really have no idea, or concern, but things had changed. No reliance on broken Haitian planes; or Haitian, Government pilots; or "Haitian" ways of getting things done. This time we had reliable USCG pilots and planes. I was elated. What a turnaround!

The operation would ultimately have its own unique set of blood pressure raising stressors, and lip biting moments, however. It couldn't be any other way in Haiti, I had long before come to understand, and to expect.

Knockout Punch, While Absorbing a Few Counter Jabs

Things were set and a plan was in place. Eliobert called on the mutually agreed upon day and I told him I had rented a room at the Hotel Montana, which by Haiti's standards, was an upscale hotel and had sufficient privacy built in. It was a suitable place for a low-profile meeting and also conducive to our own tactical operational plan. It was a beautiful structure built on the side of a mountain leading up to the more upscale city of Petionville. The hotel was sadly reduced to rubble during the destructive, killer earthquake of 2010, where an estimated 230,000 people died, according to Haitian Government reporting. Eliobert agreed to the discrete meeting location and the simple arrangement involving just the two of us. Discrete and quiet was the picture that was projected. The actual, not so discrete, nor quiet, event was set for the following day, a middle of the week day, at 10:00 am.

It was bright and sunny on the early autumn day, which for all the myriad problems the country had, weather was hardly ever one of them. It was the one consistent blessing Haiti enjoyed amid the poverty and suffering it endured throughout its history. The Caribbean Island had ideal weather, unless of course it became the target of an occasional hurricane, earthquake, or some other calamity. Eliobert showed up right on time and knocked on the hotel room door where I was waiting. Our surveillance team was discreetly in place, out of sight. Eliobert entered the pleasant looking room with its inviting hardwood floors and wall trim. The name Montana suited the décor nicely. We took our seats at a polished wooden table that could serve as a desk, across from each other, as we exchanged pleasantries.

The plan was to have him come into the room, sit down and engage in some conversation for about five minutes to get him comfortable and relaxed. We did talk for a minute or two. I was impressed and intrigued by his quiet and reserved demeanor which was very much in contrast to his rather robust projection of confidence and sturdy appearance. Our conversation was cordial and I was enjoying the moment of getting to know him a little when, prematurely I thought, the mellow encounter was suddenly and violently interrupted by Sam and his brother bursting into the room, guns drawn.

Eliobert didn't even look all that shocked when Sam, smaller in size but apparently strong enough, slammed him to the floor and quickly secured him in handcuffs. Sam had pretty good cop moves for a computer specialist. I was a little surprised at the sudden fierceness of Sam's take down and told him to take it easy. There was no need for violence. Eliobert did not look like he wanted to resist.

Maybe my distaste to the over reaction was because of the sudden interruption of what was turning into a rather pleasant conversation with the notorious drug kingpin, who came across so mild mannered. I actually wished for a little more time to talk to him because he had the demeanor of someone who was serious about having a real conversation; and I was sincerely interested in getting to know him a little, and hearing what he had to say about Haiti's drug trafficking situation. I didn't have a clue what he might have wanted to say, but I felt mildly disappointment at the lost opportunity and time that was suddenly snatched away. In that moment, watching the proud man who projected a certain dignity, hit the floor, I felt a twinge of pity for him. Maybe because I had so thoroughly set him up and snookered him, combined with the sudden violent assault he did not deserve. My impulse was to tell him I was sorry, but I held that momentary sentiment in check. I sensed we could have become friends on different terms, in different circumstances, but this was our reality, and my job.

I did, however, feel a sense of accomplishment when I took the phone to inform the USCG officer, Captain Mike, at the Embassy that he could inform the Coast Guard Air Wing Station in Miami that we had Eliobert in custody, and they could now launch their plane to come and pick him up. That would entail a little over two hours of waiting. Under normal circumstances that would not have posed a problem but, there were goblins hiding in the closet that decided it was time for a Halloween Horror Thriller to happen. The goblins created unforeseen obstacles for us. The two hours wait for the plane would turn into a harrowing, nightmarish experience, and would prove to be anything but boring.

Part III | Change, Challenge, and Conquest

Trouble on the Trip to Takeoff

Eliobert was seated in the back of Sam's car along with Sam's brother, a special operations cop. Herman was with me in mine. We took the longer route to the Airport, through Petionville, to avoid the congestion of Port-au-Prince proper, and the tortuously slow and often totally stalled traffic through the downtown area. We drove up the hill, away from the city center area. As we began our descent from peaceful Petionville, travelling the "back way" toward the airport, we encountered what appeared to resemble something akin to a scene from hell.

Tires and other debris were set on fire, blocking off the route. The sight of protesters was evident, in typically good Haitian form, creating the now familiar depiction of major mayhem; with billowing, ominous plums of black smoke filling the air. Herman, was driving the Land Rover that he and I occupied, leading the way. Sam, Eliobert and Sam's brother were following. I had an awful sinking feeling deep in my digestive apparatus, very much linked to my central nervous system. All my sensory predictors screamed in unison, trouble ahead! It all culminated in something feeling like a punch in the gut. It was a crippling onslaught of adrenalin overload that was becoming all too familiar these days. The "Haitian Sensation," was beginning to boil over.

A convergence of the mental and nervous system adrenalin onslaughts, clashing with the opposing face of peace and harmony, always seemed to be doing battle with each other; like the X-Games in extreme sports. These moments of dissonance were both exhilarating and addictive. All my life I had been, for better or worse, attracted to the merging of these opposing magnetic pulls on my center of gravity. The adrenalin rush, and exhilaration it produced, sometimes a little out of balance with the peace and harmony I sought, created that conflict. I think my nervous system was experiencing some serious pinging that day. I would later reflect on this attraction to the adrenalin highs and question what impact it might have had on my general health, physically and mentally, more so physically, but the two go hand in hand. This was the way I was wired from very early on in life, or before I was born, written into my genetic code. So, there is no blame directed at anyone, including myself, or God. It is just the way I happen to be put together, "incredibly and wonderfully made," but imperfect, as we all are, for now.

Eliobert had a plan B, as William had with the portentous flight to Miami, it appeared. It was a cunning one that he apparently concocted in the event he was arrested, thereby putting in place a bit of an insurance plan. No assurance, but if he were taken, he could potentially escape with help from the minions of loyal beneficiaries of his benevolence and favors over time. He probably also had his own people at the Hotel Montana conducting counter surveillance, discretely watching to see what would happen to him. Good plan. Any smart crook would have. Police are not the only ones who think about surveillance.

There was probably also a certain element of the populous present who were just attracted to rioting and creating chaos, for whatever the reason. It's a Haitian thing. Or maybe just a human thing. The fires grew huge and our route to the airport appeared to be totally blocked. We seemed to be stuck, as were my feelings of optimism about reaching our destination. What had been only imagined ghosts of threatening scenarios in the Ketant fiasco; this time around, the threat of tangible trouble was very real and very visible. Herman managed to navigate around the first blaze, which obscured our view with the billowing mountains of black smoke, but then we appeared to be encircled and totally blocked by the bedlam as we drew closer to the airport. We seemed to be surrounded, and stuck with nowhere to go. All my sensory faculties were being blown up. Focus, laugh if you can, it helps. So, Herman and I did just that. That's the sign of a great partner.

My guardian angel must have been with me that day once again, as well as many of his friends. As my mind was scrambling in high gear and in a state of semi panic trying to think positive thoughts about how to escape the mess; out of no-where, there suddenly appeared a massive law enforcement presence in unmarked black SUVs with lights flashing all around. The very large persuasive, police presence was managing to open up enough space for us to somehow pass through the hellish chaos. Some of the numerous rioters were positioned at the entrance to the airport access road, which they were attempting to close off. Overriding that roadblock and suddenly dominating the situation was a small army of huge intimidating looking human beings, who were serious and intentional, possibly from the Palace Security Detail. It felt to me more likely from heaven. Maybe Sam had a role to play with his palace connections. He didn't comment, I didn't ask.

I am not sure who they were or where they came from. They did not look like typical HNP officers. Very big guys donned in black riot gear, determined in their objective, which was very visible in their serious demeanor. They were a very welcome sight which planted a smile as big as they were on my face. Herman and I laughed, once more.

Why they showed up as our timely saviors I still wonder about to this day, but my thankful response and feeling of relief eclipsed any curiosity at the time. They were possibly called in to clear the airport entrance for just general commerce considerations as the rioters were attempting to block entrance to the airport, or possibly they were called by someone to assist with our operation. I don't know and I never inquired, but at the time it didn't matter. They appeared as angels dressed in black, and really big ones at that. They were there and they saved us, and that's all that mattered at the moment.

From that version of Hell, we made it onto the airport property safely, Eliobert intact. That was another unexpected miracle in a series of miracles that seemed to be happening all too frequently, in stark contrast to the normal, natural order of Haitian events. They were occurring all around, at every turn these days. I was okay with that, and thankful as well. I stashed the thought away in my mind for something to ponder later.

We had a little time to kill before the USCG plane arrived, but not too long. We had spent more than the better part of an hour navigating our way through Haitian hell on the trip down from Petionville, which normally would have only taken minutes. The Coast Guard "Fly Boys," as my friend Mark used to not so affectionately refer to them, were impressively prompt. I was relieved that we had a somewhat secure and private location within the confines of the airport available to us to wait in, to the extent that there really was any security or privacy in Haiti.

When the plane arrived, two DEA agents from Miami deplaned, and enormous relief finally set in at the welcome sight. My guys were here to help and lift this load of anxiety from my shoulders. They took Eliobert into custody, swiftly put him on the plane, and without a moment's hesitation, the plane departed. No slow-motion taxi down the runway this time. It was fast and sleek. Slick work, was my thought at the beautiful sight of the quick and fluid coordination of moving bodies and sharp looking plane; and the victorious cinemograph they produced together. Smooth as a ballet on stage, and a salve for stress, the relief of which probably made it look more surreal than it really was. Dream scenes are sometimes okay in real life. We had a moment of sober celebration, or maybe just one of quiet relief that it all turned out well in the end. The job was done. Another stress-free day at the office in Port-au-Prince came to its conclusion with an accompanying feeling of accomplishment to be deeply savored, once again. Thankful . . . but tired now.

26

A Dream Come True, a Country Changed

The impact on Haiti's drug trade with the capture and delivery of Ketant to the US Justice system, and the subsequent arrest of Eliobert, was huge and had an even bigger impact than what I could have ever dreamed. These events with the resultant cooperation of the two Kingpin traffickers, miraculously opened the flood gates for future prosecutions of many high-level narcotics traffickers and complicit government officials. The events seemed to transform Haiti's posture with regard to cooperation with US law enforcement overnight. They had a significant impact on what DEA could accomplish in Haiti with the remainder of uncorrupted members of the Haitian National Police. The tide had turned, and at least in this moment in the country's history, there was a dramatic turn for the good. The Government began to cooperate with the DEA, resulting in numerous indictments and high-level prosecutions in the U.S. I can only imagine that Aristide had been forced to cover for his own misdeeds and was compelled to put on a new face. It was probably too late for him, however. The narco-political landscape of the country had changed overnight, and a new era had begun, at least for the present moment in its history. The future had its own landscape, but not mine to deal with or worry about.

As reported in an article appearing in the Miami Herald on Wednesday, September 22, 2004: "A major Haitian drug defendant (Eliobert Jasme), who is helping federal agents investigate alleged trafficking in deposed President Jean-Bertrand Aristide's administration, is expected to plead guilty on cocaine-smuggling charges, according to sources familiar with the case." Eliobert faced 10 years to life in prison, a $4 million fine, and an unspecified amount of restitution to be made based on what he was charged with. A plea deal and unrestrained cooperation was his best option. He would plead guilty to two conspiracy charges in the agreement and be sentenced to 10 years. Eliobert, over time had smuggled roughly 300 tons of cocaine from Colombia through Haiti, which was destined for the U.S., as disclosed by his own admission.

According to the same article, with the cooperation of Eliobert and Ketant, who admitted to paying Aristide and his former head of Presidential Palace Security up to $500,000 a month to let them land planes loaded with cocaine, from Colombia, on the specially constructed highway just outside of Port-au-Prince. Numerous other Haitian officials were ultimately implicated and indicted. They included people with whom I had dealings during my time in Haiti, including Jean Nesly Lucien, National Police Director; my buddy Rudy Therassan, National Police Commander; Evintz Brillant, Haitian anti-drug chief (BLTS); and Romaine Lestin, former Port-au-Prince Airport Police Commander.[1] Not the least of these was my former friend Guy Phillipe. Other major drug traffickers, not mentioned here, were also caught in the ever-widening web.

The small snow ball, which at the beginning of its decent down the mountain of corruption, had rapidly turned into an avalanche of tumbling snow crashing down, finally came to a halt at the bottom, on its own depleted inertia of criminality. Melting now, it was transformed into a river of cleansing, free running water, reflecting a glimmer of light on the stream, following its pull in the right direction. A good moment in time, a gigantic institutional culture change had suddenly occurred in the swiftness of the unforeseen avalanche, set off by the small, but deadly disturbance of greed.

Time to Say Goodbye

In my world of the Good, the sometimes Bad, and sometimes Ugly; it seemed there was nothing much left for me to do in Haiti. The most notorious of the Haitian drug traffickers were in U.S. Federal custody and with their cooperation it remained to be seen if the boom would be lowered on President Aristide. It was an intriguing thought to consider. At best he could potentially be indicted by a federal grand jury. At the least he would be exposed for the financial gain he amassed by allowing Haiti to become the

---

1. Miami Herald, Article by Jay Weaver, *Haitian Drug Suspect to Plead Guilty*, September 22, 2004.

significant transshipment country it had become. I would just have to wait and see how things worked out. There was nothing more I could do in my position to substantially have any impact on his future status as president, more than what I had already done. I had set the bar pretty high with my goal of changing the country, but with grace from the Creator of things, made that jump and cleared the height for a personal best, in track parlance. It was a cooperative effort between God and me, I was sure. But the mission had been accomplished in my tiny view of the world.

When the dust had settled and all the reporting was complete, I just felt it was time to leave Haiti, a place I had grown comfortable to live and do my work in. I had developed a fondness for the country and the people. My wife had also grown to find comfort in our surroundings. Maybe that is just a result of familiarity, but that breeds closeness and a certain bonding. My goals, however, had been achieved. I couldn't make this place my home, although having Haiti's weather surrounding my permanent residence would not be disagreeable to my taste. We had been there nearly five years which was more than the two tours I had signed up for. But I accomplished what had become a passion of mine, once I finally got my grounding and solid footing there.

It was an amazing experience to reflect on; how things and events had so dramatically turned to a positive direction during the nearly five years there. I felt, in this time of reflection, a sense of deep, satisfying accomplishment, and gratitude for how events had suddenly turned in my favor and finally into success. I honestly felt as though there had been a powerful guiding force far beyond my ability to see or understand at work, orchestrating things in amazing ways with other-worldly timing. Of course, it had to involve my cooperation, but something much bigger, like a Mover behind the scenes, directing things to fall into perfect place. It was both a gratifying and mystifying experience to ponder in quiet moments of reflection.

But along with it all, I also felt a little bit of melancholy, a letdown after an exhilarating, adrenalin charged, five years high; like a victory in a big athletic contest that required years of training. But this was bigger than any I had ever experienced before. What next(?) . . . is the natural question to ask in the search for authentic. I was quite sure at this point that I did not need any more adrenalin induced highs, however. Those chemical releasing stores in my brain were now running very low on reserves.

Closure

There was one order of business left—the party prior to parting, and celebration of our success. Our office was now on the map and there was little doubt there were accolades being bantered about in our Puerto Rico, Regional Headquarters, and in DEA Headquarters, in Washington D.C. After all, we had brought to justice, two of DEA's Kingpin targets in just a matter of a few months. And as a bonus thrown in to the deal, it changed the face of the country's narco-political, U.S. relational landscape. No small feat in the environment that was Haiti at that time. The odds were not in our favor, but the miraculous way in which people and events gelled in nearly perfect harmony, the impossible became a reality in story book fashion. We had reason to celebrate, and that we did, leaving me in the mildly embarrassing condition of having to be driven home at the conclusion of the very warm and cohesive social event that took place at Al's house. Better safe than leaving the country with a smudge on the glitter that had been cast. Besides, sometimes a little humility is a good thing when you errantly believe you have the skill of a race car driver, who shouldn't consider driving himself, in a moment of post victory-celebration-delirium. One best not even try. Prudence served me better, but it was more Al's than mine, I have to admit.

A few days before our departure, my trustworthy and brave friend Sam arrived at our residence in a pick-up truck, along with a couple helpers that he had co-opted. They unloaded from the bed of the truck a nearly life-sized statue of the famed and revered, Haitian General, and self-proclaimed Emperor, Jean-Jacques Dessalines, and presented it to me as a farewell gift. Dessalines was a leader in the Haitian Revolution and the first ruler of independent Haiti. Under Dessalines, Haiti became the first country in the Americas to permanently abolish slavery.

Sam's gracious gift was a heartwarming one that immediately struck an emotional chord. It was a heartfelt symbol that reflected his deep appreciation for, and understanding of what impact our victory together had achieved in the battle over the evil of corruption that had gripped the country in a choke hold in recent years. Drawing on the symbolic correlation of oppression to freedom, in the context of slavery that the people of Haiti had endured under oppressive French colonization, ultimately gaining freedom; versus the liberation from corruption in the current day, was not lost on me, and spoke clearly of Sam's depth and cultural, historical appreciation for the country's past and present.

Dessalines was initially designated Governor-General, but was later elevated to the status of Emperor, and was bestowed the name Jacques I, in 1804, by the generals of the Haitian Revolution. He is regarded as one of the founding fathers of Haiti, having served as an officer in the French army when they were fending off Spanish and British incursions, but later rose to become a commander in the revolt against France itself. After defeating the French, Dessalines ordered the massacre of between 3,000 and 5,000 French settlers in Haiti, allowing other white non-French nationals to stay and live. The slaughter of the French settlers in Haiti's infancy causes me to wonder if that inaugural event somehow might have set a tone for the country's ensuing history of violent political troubles throughout its history, up to the present day. He was a champion of Haiti's freedom, but also may have established its character.

The statue of J. J. Dessalines was a fine piece of art work, and a touching gesture to gift the symbol representing so much meaning and history. But it seemed to weigh well in excess of one hundred pounds, and was really an unmanageable piece of décor for my wife and I to handle. The following day, grateful and moved as I was, I asked Sam to come and pick it up, explaining that we just couldn't manage it in the subsequent moves we would have to make. Generous and meaningful as Sam's gift was, and I was touched by it, was just too huge, and too bulky to carry around with us. I don't know what he, or someone, had spent to buy that replica and symbol of Haitian heroism, but we did take a picture of it for posterity and warm memory's sake.

When my wife and I departed Haiti for good this time, it was with bitter sweet emotion. I was leaving a lot of myself there, and also friends that had been made over those potent years rife with absurdity, complexity, perplexity, and grace.

Farewell to Hispaniola and Our Home Known as Haiti

We had flown to Miami many times during our nearly five years in Haiti. It was always fun to get back to the States for meetings or a small respite, but it was likewise always nice to come back to Haiti in order to re-engage in what eventually had become my passion and commitment. I had acquired meaning and purpose in my work, with a goal that may have seemed fanciful, but I had become focused on that fancy and it was a great motivator to stay the course.

Our lives as diplomats in Haiti provided us with the perks and relative comfortable living conditions, despite being surrounded by so much poverty, which was always hard for me to reconcile. There was also the violence, danger and other risks but we had been able to adjust to its realities. We did what we could in small charitable ways to alleviate some of the suffering. My wife paid a price in contracting tuberculosis while giving love to little ones left in orphanages. She spent the better part of a year semi-quarantined in Florida getting well again.

The Island of Hispaniola did have its beautiful places that would be missed. On our weekend afternoon trips driving up the mountain, we were provided some splendid vistas to rest our eyes on. The further we ascended the mountain, the less evidence of squalor we saw; giving way to some very beautiful vistas and sights, dwellings, and French styled structures of different varieties. The drives south to the city of Leogane, on the southern coast of the island, was always a pleasant excursion that offered scenic views of a much more serene, peaceful, and better-preserved Haiti; adding in a substantial mixture of its art influenced culture. A different world, different culture, and a quiet, peaceful respite; although still quite poor.

The "Haitian sensation" was about to come to its permanent conclusion, with all its challenges and intrusive body blows of adrenaline rushes, which I had probably become too familiar with. That, mixed with its intermittent experiences of rich relationships and beauty, was a cocktail I would miss. On the other hand, I was somewhat looking forward to the new chapter which awaited us in Los Angeles, where I had asked to be transferred to. I had a brother and his family living there and looked forward to being able to get together with them. Joe was a cop on the Santa Monica Police Department at the time, so with the commonality in professional undertaking, we could share stories and talk about "stuff." We had a somewhat deeper, more spiritual compatibility that always made it pleasurable to be around and talk to him. So, on the precipice of our departure from Haiti, there were a plethora of feelings and emotions swimming through my stream of consciousness, like fish in the deep ocean, swimming fast through their liquid space, in fast changing directions.

Sam and Renaud saw us off at the airport. As we flew away from Port-au-Prince, while straining for a final look out the window at the bright blue waters of the Caribbean below, and the majestic view of the mountains in retreat of our view, I felt a pang of nostalgia in that moment of leaving the island. It was the middle of the month, November, 2003. A lot had happened in the very recent past, and things were going to pick up steam as a result of our work on that Western third of the Island known as Hispaniola. I took one long final look at the scenery fading in the background. The vice like grip of corruption choking the Country, bleeding its civil dignity, had been broken, and the wheels of a new kind of liberation had been unlocked to freely turn and increase revolutions and speed; as was the 747, Boeing jet airliner I was on. I smiled in that moment of departure, moving into the unknown once again.

The Coup d'état Now, the Real Deal

Just two months after I had departed Haiti, my enigmatic friend Guy Phillipe returned in tornadic fashion and flair, leading a small army headed for

Port-au-Prince. Guy intended to take control of the country. He and his band of mutineers had taken over and already controlled many of the towns in the northern part of the country. They had advanced their political transformational movement, with a show of force and determination, to within 25 miles north of the Capital.

In the meantime, Ketant and Eliobert were in Miami cooperating with DEA agents and the US Justice Department, laying bare everything about Aristide's involvement in Haiti's substantial drug trafficking industry. Instead of indicting Aristide, based on Ketant's and other testimony, someone high up in the U.S. Government must have delivered a strong and compelling argument that the President would be much better off just leaving Haiti rather than face a possible indictment, which would not be good for him or the country. Under all the mounting potential legal pressures, having no other real alternative, combined with Guy and his militia bearing down on the Capital, Aristide prudently resigned the presidency on February 29, 2004, and flew to the Central African Republic on a chartered plane.

His claim was that a U.S. backed coup d'état forced him from office, but that was clearly not the case. Aristide made his own bed of dirt which he in the end could not dig himself out of. Guy Philippe's look alike coup d'état never came to full fruition; because it didn't need to. Driving out Aristide was Guy's primary ambition and purpose, by means of forceful removal and replacement. But the reality was that Aristide's sudden departure occurred coincidentally by way of his own self-inflicted demise and destruction. Guy's goal was met with no blood spilled. Aristide was gone.

Boniface Alexandre, President of Haiti's Supreme Court, assumed the role of interim president, in accord with Haiti's constitution. UN peacekeeping forces swiftly descended on the island to protect its citizens. I felt victorious once again, as I received the news while at my office in Los Angeles. Guy and I had a similar goal but for different reasons, or maybe not so different. I thought Aristide was a bad character and a criminal. Guy may have just wanted the President's job. I really don't know for sure, but nonetheless, a mutually sought-after result had been achieved for both of us in the end. Aristide, fallen from grace into the arms of corruption, was out. Case closed.

Congressional Silliness on Display

Aristide's claim that the US had backed a coup to force him from office was taken up in US Congressional hearings shortly thereafter. On March 9, 2004 Congresswoman Barbara Lee (D-Cal), Congressional Black Caucus Haiti Task Force Co-Chair, introduced H.R. 3919, The Truth Act

(The Responsibility to Uncover the Truth about Haiti). It called for an independent bipartisan commission to uncover the facts about the Bush Administration's involvement in the recent "coup d'état" in Haiti. The bill was co-sponsored by Haiti Task force Co-Chair John Conyers and 23 other House members.

"The Truth ACT" called for the commission to investigate, among other questions, the following:

1. Did the U.S. Government impede democracy and contribute to the overthrow of the Aristide government?
2. Under what circumstances did President Jean-Bertrand Aristide resign, and what was the role of the U.S. Government in bringing about his departure?
3. To what extent did the U.S. impede efforts by the international community, particularly the Caribbean Community (CARICOM) countries, to prevent the overthrow of the democratically-elected Government of Haiti?
4. What was the role of the United States in influencing decisions regarding Haiti at the United Nations Security Council and in discussions between Haiti and other countries that were willing to assist in the preservation of the democratically-elected Government of Haiti by sending security forces to Haiti?
5. Was U.S. assistance provided or were U.S. personnel involved in supporting, directly or indirectly, the forces opposed to the government of President Aristide?
6. Was U.S. bilateral assistance channeled through nongovernmental organizations that were directly or indirectly associated with political groups actively involved in fomenting hostilities or violence toward the government of President Aristide?"

"The Bush Administration's efforts in the overthrow of a democratically-elected government must be investigated," Lee said. "All of the evidence brought forward thus far suggests that the Administration has, in essence, carried out a form of 'regime change,' a different variation than it took in Iraq, but still a regime change. The American people and the international community deserve to know the truth, and this bill will offer the opportunity to investigate the long-term origins of the overthrow of the Haitian government and the impact of our failure to protect democracy."[2] Politics!

---

2. Library of Congress, H.R. 3919, Rep. Barbara Lee, (D-Cal), March 9, 2004.

So much pompous posturing, it becomes laughable to the point of nausea. Does Congress ever look beyond politics for the truth? Apparently not. They had the facts, and if not, shame on them. Was it on record, even though classified at the time? Sure, but they have clearances to access the truth. The US Government had not forced Aristide from his elected office. Aristide made his own bed. And by crawling into it, and even nurturing big time drug traffickers as bed partners, he was making millions of dollars for the pleasure of sleeping in it. This political Congressional pomposity made me sad, and laugh simultaneously. There was likely more than ample evidence to indict Aristide at the time he resigned. He had made the regression from "Priest and Reformer," to "Corrupt and Criminal," in a relatively short span of time. A dramatic reversal of salvation protocol, I sense. But prosecutors, siding with their own sense of prudent motives, chose not to indict him. I was fine with that. Aristide was exposed and his corrupting influence vanquished. Haiti had yet another opportunity to get it right.

The US Government did Aristide a favor by suggesting he just leave the country, and his office, before something worse happened to him. Nor would it have been good for the people of Haiti if he were indicted in the U.S., or to have a bloody showdown in the streets of Port-au-Prince with a threatening militia, intent on ousting him, knocking at his door. His best option was to just leave and call it a day. With Guy Philippe and his militia staged just outside Port-au-Prince, poised to pounce on the Capital, who knows what the outcome might have been. Probably not a pretty scenario.

After the Story

I received an interesting, rather mysterious phone call while at work, living life in my new world at the Los Angeles, High Intensity Drug Trafficking Area (HIDTA) office. I was assigned to an enforcement group largely made up of Los Angeles Police Department, narcotics officers and detectives. The voice on the other end of the line introduced himself as an intelligence officer with the Department of Defense. He and his partner wanted to fly to L.A., to interview me about my experience with certain people in Haiti and get my take on the country's political environment in the wake of Aristide's abrupt departure. The country was in its more typical state of chaos again, and there was no lack of jockeying for position in the sudden power vacuum left by him.

It was a bright sunny day in the suburban city of Westwood, where I met with my visitors on the veranda of a posh hotel near Hollywood. It was interesting; they wanted to talk to me about Guy Philippe, in an attempt to gain some sense of what sort of character he was, if he was to ascended to some kind of power figure within the shifting struggle for that deity in Haiti. During its history, especially in the modern era, the U.S. had long kept a trained eye on political events in Haiti with the express purpose and intention of trying to maintain stability in the volatile country. It was in the U.S.'s national security interest to maintain stability in the Caribbean region, and Haiti was a perpetual problem in that arena.

Guy had successfully engineered a nearly *fait complete coup d'état,* and laid claim to leadership status in the country shortly after I departed. His rising populism gaining momentum, contributed to some of the factors which applied persuasive pressure on Aristide to abruptly leave Haiti. Things were now a mess again in Haiti's political, landscape, and the US Marines were back once again to ensure that bedlam did not resurface and become, once again. the normative narrative of the day.

The gentlemen from DOD and I had a nice talk for a couple of hours in the quiet space of the outdoor terrace at the hotel, while taking in the pleasant warmth of the Southern California afternoon sun on that February afternoon. The over-arching theme of the briefing with the two intelligence operatives was discussion concerning the massive corruption metastasizing at the core of the country's political structure. A history re-told. I told them what I could about Guy Philippe, which was not a whole lot other than he was a gifted, charismatic character who I thought had an abundance of talent. But I could not vouch for his virtues or character, because I just didn't know him that well. There was a lot of chatter when I was in Haiti that Guy was also complicit in facilitating the drug trade in the north part of the country where, as Commander, he had control of the police. I never got to know him that well though, because of where he worked and resided. I had most likely saved his life by a thin hair when he was forced to abruptly flee the country, so we weren't afforded the opportunity to really get to know each other all that well. When the DOD guys were satisfied that I had given them my best accounting of political tendencies in Haiti, they left. And that was the last of any official involvement I had with the country, which I somehow now missed.[3]

---

3. There had been numerous reports put out in journalistic and reported articles during the time frame of Aristide's departure from office and the arrest of Jacques Ketant. Kyle Swenson's journalistic account in "The Rise and Fall of Jacques Ketant" is an excellent and compelling story. However, much of the reporting I have read misses the mark in accurate accounting of events. I therefore refer the readers of such accounts to the story as is told in these previous pages. I was there as participant, and in many ways, "engineer" of the process, and was as fully engaged as my life allowed me to be.

PART IV

In Search of the Unseen;
Locating that Pearl of Great Value

27

Life After Slaying the Dragon

I spent a year with the LA cops before getting promoted. I finished out my career over the next several years managing the Asset Forfeiture program for DEA's Los Angeles Division, which included overseeing those operations in LA; Riverside; Las Vegas; Reno, Nevada; Hawaii, and Guam. I was more than satisfied to just be a manager, and at this stage on the career trajectory, happy to forfeit any more opportunities for excitement and adrenalin inducing adventures. Now I dealt with systems, people, and legal issues; which at this point in my career suited me just fine. I had had enough thrills and spills of challenging adventure, drama episodes, and excitement for a lifetime. Now I was ready for steady, but I still had a yearning for something that was elusive, not able to put my finger on what exactly that was. There was an itch somewhere in my psyche and my soul.

I thought that maybe pursuing a master's degree in Theology, which had always been an inherent interest, might help fill that "wanting something more" feeling that was stirring in me, deep down in those depths of soul we do not regularly access. I needed to dive deeper into life's core meaning and search for what had not yet been more completely uncovered in those unexplored caverns of the soul, yet to be fully excavated. What did it mean to exist as a being, a person alive, to breath, think, love, and live dreams dreamed? Now I can say with some certainty, that the immutable, implanted, naked desire for a sense of completeness or wholeness, is that which is our deepest desire. It is that spark of the Divine planted in the soul, beckoning us toward just that end. Well, just maybe pondering such things in the proper environment might provide some clues as to what this unsatiated thirst might be clamoring for. Living in a real-life action movie had not quite provided the answer I was in search of. Although it was a blast, and I would not have traded a moment of it; although some moments, admittedly, I would have, but that just goes for life in general.

I reflect back on the advice of the psychiatrist family friend, who instructed me in my parents' living room in our house on the Mississippi River in Minnesota years before, that I was too sensitive to work in law enforcement. He may not have been incorrect, but with stronger urgings tugging on me in my search for identity and fulfillment, I did not heed his professional assessment, and charged off into the dream with its more attractive colors. I'm grateful that I took the matter under my own advisement. In fact, if John were alive today, I would present my argument to him that being sensitive in my chosen line of work was in fact a huge advantage in achieving success. Without the "sensitive" tools of empathy and being innately able to understand and respect others, as people made in the image of God, even criminals; there wouldn't have been too much chance for success. My career was built on exactly that. Being sensitive and able to relate to other human beings as sacred creatures. It was the conduit for success in ways I never really thought about in my early musings. That career craving for the "wild side" of things now satisfied, a new avenue with new sights to be gazed at, and considered, was beckoning.

Leaning Forward into Proper Order and Posterity

I inquired into the master's degree program at Loyola Marymount University, and applied. After a somewhat pleasant, panel interview, I was accepted by the Department of Theological Studies and began my new quest. It would take about three and a half years to complete on a schedule that would be compatible with working full time. It would entail a lot of work and focus, but I felt driven, in search of something to fill a void in my heart and mind. Except for the cost, it worked out very well, and set me on a path of discovery that helped satisfy the thirst for "that something more" feeling that was gnawing at me. Additionally, I suppose, realizing the final chapter with DEA was drawing nearer to being written, left me with a feeling and desire for something new to chew on. I had a craving to "go deeper" into the meaning of it all. Where it would lead to, I did not know. I had satisfied that natural male craving for adventure, and a battle to engage in, genetically programmed into my DNA identity by the Creator of such things. I had fought my battles on the field, and in the process found my "Beauty" to rescue. At this particular stage in life's journey, I was okay with just reflecting on it all, and on life itself.

After our five-year "honeymoon" in Haiti, while still living and working in Los Angeles, I received an annulment from my previous marriage, granted by the Catholic Diocese of Los Angeles. My current marriage to my "Burmese Beauty," although not ethnic Burmese, was "con validated" at Holy Angels Catholic Church in Arcadia, California, by none other than my friend of old, Blasé, who was now the bishop in Rapid City, South Dakota. I had always known he was going places in his vocational calling. He never wavered in his focus or purpose.

Blasé graciously reached out to me with a surprising phone call I received from him one evening. I had recently visited with him when the Diocese of St. Paul, and Minneapolis Bishops, converged in California for their annual retreat. The serene venue was set at a beautiful retreat center, near where we lived, in the foothills of the San Gabriel Mountains.

During the ensuing phone conversation, he offered to come back to Los Angeles, on a yet to be established date, to preside over the sacramental ceremony of having our marriage blessed, and made copacetic in the eyes of the Church. As a friend he apparently wanted to get me set straight in the Catholic way, and went way out of his own way in order to do so; and at the same time, place his personal stamp on that process. Blasé has since moved on to a greater role in the Church, as he is now known as Cardinal Blasé Cupich, and serves as the Arch Bishop for the Diocese of Chicago. For those wondering what "con validation" means; it is in simple terms, just having a marriage blessed in the Church, like as the sacrament of Matrimony itself, being codified in Catholic Church annuls.

A few months later, after having completed the Right of Christian Initiation for Adults (RCIA), Sweet was baptized a Catholic at the same church in Arcadia, California. My brother Joe, and his wife, who live in the Los Angeles area, were her sponsors. I now refer to her in religious affiliation terms as a "Buddhist Catholic." You don't erase a person's culture and inculcated upbringing overnight for the sake of "correct" religious appropriation, terminology, or appearance. Human beings are far too complex to fit into a neatly wrapped box. She is her own unique, complex configuration of beautifully imagined, and wonderful blend of biological and spiritual creation; with her own personal life experience, making her the beautiful person she is. That said, she is her own unique person, as are all human beings.

Now our ticket was appropriately punched for purposes of proper church protocol. I'm not sure if it all had much impact on my salvation in the eternal view of things, but it squared things up in the Catholic sense, and probably made my very Catholic mom happy too.

Pointing North

I felt satisfied that I had accomplished what I thought was my natural vocational calling in life, at least where my instincts had led me; to fight a battle, conquer the world (at least my small part of it), and rescue a beauty. All my natural male inclinations found their fulfillment during the course of my law enforcement career. There had been dazzling heights ascended to, and cavernous regions blindly stumbled into. Experiences lived well, or not so well, were lived nonetheless; and were more than what I had expected in the end. It was good, and I want to believe that along the way, I might have contributed to humanity in some way, using the talents God had bestowed on me for that reason and purpose. I trust that in some fashion I did. There are indeed many measures for success in the world, and most of them in the end, are meaningless. But my hope is that my small contribution to the Grand Plan would not be counted in that category.

In striving to fulfill those fanciful yearnings, yet very real innate urgings of the heart, I had done so, to the extent that I lived out my dream of slaying dragons that appeared on the path of my life; while hopefully accomplishing some good along the way, navigating the road that had been paved for me. In rescuing my "beauty," I discovered human love in marriage, yet the desire for something more remained. Something deeper, something I can't clearly define, lingered within me clamoring for attention to find its' expression. In Saint Augustine's timeless words: "You have made us for yourself, O God, and our hearts are restless until they rest in you;" I believe is the answer and precise antidote for that elusive, restless churning in my soul. It is also applicably so, and the answer for all people of good will who are in "search" of their deepest longing, I might respectfully submit.

In his book, *The Soul's Upward Yearning: Clues to Our Transcendent Nature from Experience and Reason*, Robert Spitzer, SJ, quotes Karl Rahner, a forceful modern-day theologian, as he sees unity and fulfillment of our transcendent nature in God's love.

> "God wishes to communicate himself, to pour forth the love which he himself is. This is the first and the last of his real plans and hence of his real world too. Everything else exists so that this one thing might be: the eternal miracle of infinite Love. And so, God makes a creature whom he can love: he creates man. He creates him in such a way that he *can* receive this Love which is God himself, and that he can and must at the same

time accept it for what it is: the ever-astounding wonder, the unexpected, unexacted gift.[1]

I've come to believe we are created with an orientation toward God, created from Love with a vocation to acknowledge and accept that love, as Rahner resonates in his rich description above. I understand that it is in the precious gift of life, and living it with gratitude for God's inestimable gift of the hoped-for experience of communal life-eternal in the Triune God; is where happiness is only to be found. His gift and our response to that "ever-astounding wonder, the unexpected, unexacted gift," is where we locate wholeness and completeness, there and only there. It is our ultimate, true happiness and fulfillment, joy, in hope.

---

1. Spitzer, *Soul's Upward Yearning*, 161. Extract from Rahner, *Foundations of Christian Faith*, 123–24.

28

The Challenge

Actions we take that direct us toward God are in accord with the imperatives of our true nature and God's design. When we open ourselves to living moral, loving lives following the example of Jesus we are not simply doing something "religious," we are fulfilling the most fundamental requirement of our nature and humanity.

In his book *Toward God,* Casey explains that through prayer one develops a more acute sense of dissatisfaction with the less desirable aspects of one's life, combined with a mysterious sense of contentment that becomes more fortified and harder to move off center—a feeling of "something going on inside," and there becomes a growing realization that one is being drawn toward God. While the two realizations seem to be opposites, they are actually pulling in the same direction, although in different ways. One way shakes us out of our complacency while the other reminds us that ultimately only God can bring us happiness.[1] This premise is very near the shore line where I have anchored my ship, and there finding a rock to plant my feet firmly on. God is where steady is. Where steady is, in still or turbulent waters, we discover peace, and in peace we find joy.

Spiritual experience has a dual nature: it is at the same time an attraction to God and a detachment, or turning away from sin (soiling our relationship with God).[2] Our attraction to God and turning toward him causes us to turn away from those attachments that deluded our understanding of

---

1. Casey, *Toward God,* 120.
2. Casey, *Toward God,* 121.

where we mistakenly thought we would find happiness; slaying dragons, adventure, creating a memorable reputation, or success. All these attractions, while not bad things are fleeting, albeit very human and legitimate natural inclinations in the human genome. However, we are called to more; to a deeper experience, an experience of God. This is where, and in what, and in whom, joy is located. "Joy is the touch of God's finger. The object of our longing is not the touch but the Toucher. This is true of all good things—they are all God's touch. Whatever we desire, we are really desiring God."[3]

In seeking and finding God amid our attractions to the world does not happen suddenly, but requires a gradual modification of attitude. While we most likely repeatedly return to our vices, after each relapse there is less satisfaction with them or attraction to them. A passage from Saint Gregory the Great describes this dynamic and how it works:

> Sometimes one is admitted to a particular, unaccustomed experience of inner sweetness and is, in some way, a new creature, set afire by the breadth of the Spirit. The more one tastes the object of love, the stronger grows one's desire for it. Within oneself one craves what one has experienced through the inner sense of taste and, from love of that sweetness, becomes of less value in one's own eyes. After one has discovered that sweetness one becomes able to perceive what sort of person one is without it. One tries to prolong the experience, but is driven back from the strength because one is still weak. And being incapable of contemplating such purity, one weeps sweet tears and falls back and lies down on the tears of one's weakness. For the eye of the mind is unable to fix itself on what it had so fleetingly glimpsed. It is subject to the constraint of inveterate habit which holds it down. In this state one is filled with yearning and ardently tries to transcend oneself, but each time one is beaten by fatigue and falls back into the familiar darkness. A soul so moved must endure a serious inner struggle against itself.[4]

My first recollection and taste of that "sweetness," which Gregory talks of, came to me in a moment of grace when I was a boy of about seven or eight years old, on a cold winter night in December. I was outdoors, by myself, on the snow-covered driveway in Minnesota with shovel in hand. It was a crystal-clear night, the sky lit up with countless bright stars in the north country. They seemed to be talking to me in their utter silence and brilliance. I was thoroughly enjoying the solitude, silence, and grandeur of

---

3. Kreeft, *Heaven: The Heart's Deepest Longing*, 156.
4. Casey, *Toward God*, 121–22; citation from Gregory the Great, *Commentary on the Book of Job*, 23.43; PL.76, col. 277–78.

the occasion. I had an overwhelming feeling of not being alone, however. Quite the contrary, I was suddenly filled with warmth and a profound peace, which in the moment took hold and filled me with awe from deep within. Joy overflowed my being and I broke into singing "*O Holy Night*," as Christmas was drawing near it seemed appropriate in the moment. At the time I did not question the origin of the feeling but was just simply grateful for it. I wanted to share the experience with someone, but don't recall if I did or not. I think not, for fear of not being understood, nor having words to describe it.

A Process

This kind of experience is not deserved or something we earn through anything we've done or are. They are moments of God visiting us on an individual level, a total free gift of the Spirit. How we accept the experience is, however, up to our inclination and will; to accept, or not, as our will and desire directs us. Darkness and greyness will certainly return because we are a fallen race since the beginning, but visitations of grace are treasures to be kept specially guarded, as gifts in our hearts for strength and maintaining the right direction on our journey moving forward, inward and upward, as the sages remind us.

Karl Rahner states that the Christian of the future will be a mystic, one who has experienced something, or he will cease to be anything at all. Wilkie Au explains that by "mysticism," Rahner does not mean singular parapsychological experiences of the Sacred but the "mysticism of daily life," the genuine experience of God emerging from the very heart of existence, being able to spot the movement of God's Spirit in the encounters of our daily life experience. Mystics, therefore, are people who have firsthand experience of God from their own personal encounter in ordinary life experience.[5]

Au, in his book *The Enduring Heart*, cites noted Old Testament biblical scholar, Walter Brueggemann, who states that spirituality is our walk with God through recurrent patterns of:

- Being securely oriented
- Being painfully disoriented
- Being surprisingly reoriented

---

5. Au and Au, *Grateful Heart*, 183–84.

This pattern repeats itself in all areas of our lives where we encounter the Divine in relation to self, others, and the world.[6]

Brueggemann's conceptual map of our earthly journey resonates with my own personal experience along the road of life's hits and misses, then hits again. I can recognize and identify these phases he describes from my personal life experience. Periods of being securely oriented are stamped with the sense of feeling secure and of well-being; success in work, loving family, financial stability, and a general sense of peacefulness. Faith comes naturally when, similar to the feeling of a fresh breeze and seeing new growth in the spring, when all of nature is being re-created and all is well. We feel secure that God is in God's heaven doing God's work out of unimaginable love for his creation in his created world. All seems good in the moment, and life is synchronized in its melodies and harmonizes in beautiful arrangements.

But experience is all too telling, when we lose these periods of synchronicity in the flash of sudden realities and moments of disruption. A whim of dissonance uninvited, a sudden illness, some discordant news or information that sets us off our footing, or something more catastrophic. It happens entirely beyond our control. It's of the human experience in our mortal world. Au says these sorts of life circumstances can dismantle the complacent sensibilities we have thus far cultivated and send us seeking. We are stripped bare and unmasked in the unfamiliar disequilibrium. It is in our nakedness when we are somehow more vulnerable to the Divine touch. Our life is then resituated and we are gratefully reoriented after a painful period of disorientation.[7]

Experiences within this cycle of faith life; orientation, disorientation, and then reorientation again, seem to appear in a mystical rhythm of life beyond our control or understanding. As my own experience has informed me, if properly grounded and attentive, the reorientation phase always reasserts itself. It occurs in mysterious and sometimes surprising ways, profound rediscoveries of orientation, out of the morass of confusion and chaos. These transformative experiences tend to generate feelings of gratitude, a natural partner joining the occasion of grace, a gift freely given.

There are experiences within Brueggemann's faith cycle theory that are too many to recount in my own life. They range from the seemingly very small, yet significant in terms of right orientation in all experience, moment to moment; to those monumental events which exact a very powerful change in life's direction. They are all consequential in the spiritual life I believe, and the small moments, in our movements throughout a day, shouldn't be kicked

---

6. Au, *Enduring Heart*, 27.
7. Au, *Enduring Heart*, 28.

to the side of the road. But the more dramatic, are also the more telling examples for clarity's sake, a few of which I can recount here.

Experience in Haiti

One larger example might be to revisit my experience in Haiti, when upon my arrival I was comfortably focused and confidently looking forward to the new adventure we were about to embark on after successfully completing language school. After a delay, I was eventually transferred to the troubled yet intriguing new opportunity in the Caribbean, with its unique culture and complexity, full of confidence and hope. It didn't take long, however, for the scene to turn ugly and against me, for reasons unknown, other than my sense that human failure to live up to God's original design for mankind was in play. It fast turned into a nightmare of disorientation and confusion in the context of professional relationships, that seemed to contain very real vexation and venom spewing from a snake pit I was unprepared to have fallen into. Never having experienced that same degree of animosity and acrimony before, I was knocked off my footing and perspective. Lost, and alone, might be an appropriate description of where I found myself on that island in the Caribbean.

I hung in there with a combination of sheer stubbornness and digging deep down into past life experiences, places I had been before; in combination with lessons acquired from my running career, focus and endurance. I also was aided by the strength and unwavering encouragement and commitment from my wife's own determination. Seemingly overnight, the dark, disconcerting scene took a dramatic turn toward a fresh new direction, suddenly turning to light which had always been there, only eclipsed by temporary shadows. The whole country suddenly took on an entirely different look in my eyes. Instead of letting the dower conditions of the impoverished land and my surroundings drag me down, I was suddenly inflated with optimism that filled me with energy and hope.

A new dawn emerged suddenly, and the landscape of my life radically changed almost instantaneously with the sudden and rather rare removal of the DEA Country Attaché. The toxic, unbreathable air which had polluted our office's environment was cleansed and now smelling much better, almost sweet to my mental olfactory senses.

I felt light as a feather and was transformed in the moment, ready to be carried by the fresh new breeze blowing in from an entirely different direction. There was singing and laughter in my heart. I was suddenly catapulted into a storybook epoch adventure. Grace? I think so.

Marriage, Dissolution, New Life

Another reflection on Brueggemann's faith cycle theory, involving a major life change in direction, would be the emerging untenable situation in my first marriage. In the very beginning there was a sense of grounded-ness and orientation. Over time, with maturing reflection, it sadly was transformed, by its very nature, into a life predicament that went from having realized I had made a colossal mistake by entering into a misguided relational commitment from the very beginning, to living in the hellish confusing world of schizophrenia and paranoia. Years of living in a kind of silent suffering grew louder, pounding against my own sense of containment and orientation. It eventually grew painful enough so as to harness sufficient courage to say enough. Disorientation did not end there, however. No matter how "right" a disillusion of marriage may be, divorce is extremely disquieting and disorienting, and a certain upheaval in one's equilibrium and self-evaluation is inevitable.

Out of that mire, however, I found my "Beauty to rescue," and real, true marital love was found. I regained my footing gradually and life became joyful again. Not without the normal growing pains and expectant apposing winds; but locating that gift amidst the messy landscape of life, love and joy were rediscovered, uncovered in brilliant colors of beauty: a reunion of joyful reorientation. God's love revealed in human relationship. A jewel to be relished and cherished.

Sudden Saving Grace of Light, in the Dark Hole of the Deep

Maybe the most dramatic story of all the stories, in context of Brueggemann's faith cycle model, was that of travelling down the path from grounded security and the success of late adolescence, with a wide world of potential set before me. Yet, from that bright pinnacle of anticipation about the future, the gradual descent began from security to non-security, to none at all, in a lightning-fast flash; from winning a scholarship at the U of M, to finding myself swimming in unknown waters of the seminary pond; and then sinking deeper into black waters near the ocean's floor without a life vest, drowning in its depths. It was an exhibition of tremendous talent for impulsiveness. I quickly stumbled blindly into a poverty and starvation program designed by myself. Having lost any sense of grounding, I found myself floundering in a non-directional course to cruise, where there was no course to follow at all. Where was I going and who was this person treading waters in the dark with no compass or sextant? I did not have an answer, nor could I even ask the question. My life's forward moving navigational system was in the swamp.

It was in this sorry state of lost, that I thought I had fallen in love with my ex-wife. I was in no place to know what falling in love was. But there it was where I found myself, confused and in the darkest of dark places I had ever experienced, unable to perceive or imagine the light needed in which to make an epic life decision.

The experience of being near death psychologically and spiritually, which could very well have led to a physical one also, was nipping at my heels. I was stuck in the mire and could not run, could barely walk. The blackness that was moving in was a thick cloud not only obscuring vision and light, but it was palpably felt, non-life. The non-life, death force was taking over control, bringing with it confusion, fear of its dark power and loss of any ability to render capable judgement over matters concerning self-care or the world around me. Minimal motivation to make any decision about everyday life matters or clear thinking was lost, rendered impotent and near impossible. Taking a step or two, eating, getting out of bed, or attending classes at school were out of normal reach. Thank God we don't have to think about breathing, that might have vanished also.

Then "The Rescue," and the peaceful unseen Being lifting me off the ground and across Snelling Avenue, in Saint Paul, Minnesota, telling me of its love and promise to care for me; and then that Presence gently setting me down on the other side of the street, on the grass no less; with assurances of unwavering Presence, Protection and Love; speaking clear words of peace, care, and assurance. Back in my room, another wave of sweet promise flooding the space with unworldly light, saturated my perception of that space with heaven's otherworldly life pulsating color and vibrance. I knew, there was only one way forward, and joy took over. As did life and direction, a renewed sense of purpose and meaning, the non-Life and darkness banished. Baby steps maybe at first, but direction was re-established and the breeze at my back was just enough, and a fine feeling to experience once again the following Spring morning as I started life over again. The sun was shining as I walked across campus to class.

A Reflection

Be still in God's light as he communicates Love to you. There is no force in the universe as powerful as his love which has no limit. It fills all of space, time and eternity. Our vision is clouded now but someday we will see him face to face and will experience fully how wide and long and deep is his love.

On a memorable morning, in the not-too-distant past, I woke up with a powerful, instantaneous feeling of joy flooding my soul. It was one of "awareness," of truth and clarity. Unable to actively move quite yet, a prayer of thanksgiving and gratitude was on my lips, in instantaneous, spontaneous recognition of the powerful and pulsating reality of having been thought into being by God, before the creation of the world. That awesome thought put a smile on my unmoving lips, even before my first sip of coffee. Not just created, but created in the image of God and the hope of heaven, there to spend eternity with Him. A feeling of wonder swept over my entire consciousness. What a total awesome undeserved gift; life in this world and eternal life in the next. "God is Love!"[8]

> You will seek me and find me; when you seek me with all your heart, 'I will be found by you, says the Lord.' Finding him is heaven. Seeking him is heaven's door. Where it comes from is God, and where it leads to is Heaven, and what it means is that God loves you so much that He wants you to share His joy, wants you in on the secret. If you believe in God, of course, you know where joy comes from, of why the Perfect Being never gets bored or boring.[9]

It has now become my focus and vocation to meet God face to face, and in many ways I have already. That is ultimately the plan of God for all those he made in his image and in whom his Spirit takes up holy residence. And in whatever capacity or way he might gift me, to ignite that same desire in others who may be in search of the Authentic and the Pearl of Great Price. It is my hope and desire that maybe in my own story as set forth in these pages, will this hope of heaven, instilled in my heart by God's grace, be discovered by those seekers in search of that *Pearl of Great Price*, and the *Authentic!*

---

8. 1 John 4:16.

9. Kreeft, *Doors in the Walls of the World*, an excerpt reproduced in revolving *Daily Catholic Wisdom* sent unsolicited on the internet.

Bibliography

Au, Wilkie. *The Enduring Heart: Spirituality for the Long Haul.* Mahwah, NJ: Paulist, 2000.
Au, Wilkie, and Noreen Cannon Au. *The Grateful Heart: Living the Christian Message.* Mahwah, NJ: Paulist, 2011.
Berenson, Alex. "Marijuana, Mental Illness, and Violence." *Imprimis* 48.1 (January 2019).
Casey, Michael. *Toward God: The Ancient Wisdom of Western Prayer.* Ligouri, MO: Triumph, 1996.
Eldredge, John. *Wild at Heart: Discovering the Secret of a Man's Soul.* Nashville: Nelson, 2001.
Feldmeier, Peter. *The Developing Christian: Spiritual Growth Through the Life Cycle.* Mahwah, NJ: Paulist, 1989 and 1993.
Kreeft, Peter. *Heaven: The Heart's Deepest Longing.* San Francisco: Ignatius, 1989.
Rahner, Karl. *Foundations of Christian Faith: An Introduction to the Idea of Christianity.* New York: Crossroads, 1982.
Spitzer, Robert, SJ. *The Soul's Upward Yearning: Clues to Our Transcendent Nature from Experience and Reason.* San Francisco: Ignatius, 2015.
Swenson, Kyle. "The Rise and Fall of Haitian Drug Lord Jacques Ketant." *Palm Beach New Times*, May 27, 2015. https://www.browardpalmbeach.com/news/the-rise-and-fall-of-haitian-drug-lord-jacques-ketant-7001667.
"History of Haiti." https://en.wikipedia.org/wiki/History_of_Haiti.

www.ingramcontent.com/pod-product-compliance
Lightning Source LLC
Chambersburg PA
CBHW051926160426
43198CB00012B/2052